CLASSIC

LATERAL
THINKING
PUZZLES

LATERAL
THINKING
PUZZLES

By Edward J. Harshman,

Des MacHale, and Paul Sloane

Illustrated by Myron Miller

Main Street
A division of Sterling Publishing Co., Inc.
New York

Library of Congress Cataloging-in-Publication Data Available

Material in this collection was adapted from

Clever Lateral Thinking Puzzles © 1997 by Edward J. Harshman
Perplexing Lateral Thinking Puzzles © 1997 by Paul Sloan and Des MacHale
Tricky Lateral Thinking Puzzles © 1999 by Paul Sloan and Des MacHale
Super Lateral Thinking Puzzles © 2000 by Paul Sloan and Des MacHale

10 9 8 7 6 5 4

© 2003 by Sterling Publishing Co., Inc.
Published by Sterling Publishing Co., Inc.
387 Park Avenue South, New York, NY 10016
Distributed in Canada by Sterling Publishing
c/o Canadian Manda Group, One Atlantic Avenue, Suite 105
Toronto, Ontario, Canada M6K 3E7
Distributed in Great Britain by Chrysalis Books Group PLC
The Chrysalis Building, Bramley Road, London W10 6SP, England
Distributed in Australia by Capricorn Link (Australia) Pty. Ltd.
P.O. Box 704, Windsor, NSW 2756, Australia

Printed in China
All rights reserved

Sterling ISBN 1-4027-1062-3

CLASSIC LATERAL THINKING PUZZLES

CONTENTS

INTRODUCTION

A man was held in a high-security prison and closely watched. His wife sent him a letter in which she asked, "Should I plant the potatoes in the garden now?" He replied, "Do not plant anything in the garden. That is where I hid the guns." A little later he received another letter from his wife saying, "Many policemen came to our house. They dug up the whole garden but they did not find anything." He wrote back, "Now is the time to plant the potatoes."

That man used lateral thinking to solve his wife's gardening problem—and so can we all. The world needs new and creative ways to problem-solve, and more and more people see lateral thinking puzzles as a way to fire up this process. Management trainers use these puzzles to force managers to check their assumptions; teachers use them to stimulate and reward children; parents use them on long journeys to amuse and challenge the family.

It is generally more fun to do these puzzles in a small group rather than trying to solve them individually. Typically they contain insufficient information for you to deduce the solution immediately. One person acts as quizmaster by reading the puzzle aloud. He or she then reads the solution silently. Others in the group ask questions to gather information, check assumptions, and test possible solutions. The quizmaster responds to questions in one of four ways: "Yes," "No," "Irrelevant," or "Please rephrase the question."

Sure, some of the situations are implausible. And yes, it is possible to come up with alternative solutions that fit the original puzzle. In fact, you can play a variation of the game where people try to think of as many alternative explanations as possible. But in general, you will get the most enjoyment from these puzzles if you keep questioning until you come up with the answer given in the book. There are clues at the end of each section to help out when you get stuck, but the best resource is always your own imagination—so attack the problem from a new direction—think laterally!

CLEVER PUZZLES

BATTY BANDITRY

WELCOME, SLASHER

Bob, a fifteen-year-old boy with a record of violent crimes, approached a screened porch. Taking out a switchblade, he cut

through every screen panel with large diagonal rips. A police officer drove by in a patrol car, saw what the boy was doing, and was pleased. Explain.

Clues: 51/Answer: 226.

SMASHED TAILLIGHTS

Later, Bob picked up a tire wrench and smashed the taillights of a car that he had never seen before. Police officers witnessed his act and arrested not him, but the owner of the car. Explain.

Clues: 47/Answer: 223.

SUPPOSED TO KILL?

A man drew a gun, pointed it at another man who was known to be totally law-abiding, and pulled the trigger. Click! The gun wasn't loaded. Everyone present, which included at least ten people, was surprised and outraged. Why was the intended victim blamed for the incident?

Clues: 49/Answer: 224.

BURNING DOWN THE BUILDING

An old apartment building caught fire. Most apartments were damaged badly, and many people were left homeless. An investigator arrived from the fire department. A shady man pulled him aside into a dark corner of the building and handed him five hundred-dollar bills. "It would be better for both of us," said the shady man, "if something went wrong with the investigation. Lose the papers, or whatever." The investigator looked at the money and protested, "But the landlord will want to file an insurance claim and need our report." "He won't mind," the shady man replied. "Be nice to other fire victims and don't ask questions." The investigator pocketed the money and conveniently forgot the case. Why did the landlord not get upset?

Clues: 32/Answer: 215.

CAUGHT IN THE ACT

A woman walked into a police station. "I want to report a pickpocket," she announced. A man staggered in behind her, his hand in her coat pocket. "Arrest that man!" she continued, pointing to him.

He was arrested, tried, and convicted of picking pockets. Why did he enter the police station in a posture that obviously suggested his crime?

Clues: 33/Answer: 215.

ARRESTED ANYWAY

Rocky Redneck carried a gun. He had a state-issued firearm permit that allowed him to do so, and he was careful to obey the law.

One day, he went to visit his relatives across the country, in another state. Rocky had a firearm permit from that state, too; and he could legally carry his gun there. He found out from the airlines that he could take his gun with him, if it was declared to the airline staff and was in checked baggage. Ever the law-abiding citizen, Rocky packed the gun in a suitcase, told the airline clerk about it, and had the suitcase checked. So why was Rocky arrested for weapons possession?

Clues: 32/Answer: 215.

HE CALLED THE POLICE

A burglar broke into a house, intending to steal from it. While still in the house, he called the police. Why?

Clues: 37/Answer: 217.

TRICKY TRANSPORT

DRIVING THE WRONG CAR

Hermie the Hermit had a car that needed repair but was still drivable. He had another car that worked fine. He drove the first car to a repair shop. To avoid asking someone else to drive him home, he had fastened his two cars together and towed one with the other. He therefore arrived at the repair shop with two cars and could easily drive away with the working car. But why did he tow the working car with the broken one, and not the other way around?

Clues: 34/Answer: 216.

A TOKEN WAIT IN A TOKEN LINE

Smart Stephanie worked in a city and took the subway to work every morning during rush hour. In the evening, also during rush hour, she took the subway home again. To use the subway, she had to put a subway token into a turnstile as she entered the station from the street. Although she was one of numerous commuters at those hours and had to stand in crowded subway cars, she never had to wait in a long line to buy tokens. Why not?

Clues: 50/Answer: 225.

SHE ARRIVED ON TIME

Daryl and Carol had arranged to meet at a coffee house but something came up. Daryl looked in the phone book, found Carol's home phone number and called her. "I know we were supposed to meet in the coffee house in two hours, but my boss called and I have to reschedule. I'm due at the office two hours from now." "That's too

bad," replied Carol, "but I can meet you at the coffee house in two minutes, if you'd like." Daryl agreed and, because he lived right across the street from it, was there in two minutes. He was content to wait. but Carol was waiting for him. "You live clear across town," noted Daryl. "How could you get here so fast?"

Clues: 46/Answer: 223.

WHAT DRAINED THE BATTERY?

Walter forgot to allow for the slowness of traffic in the rain and was late for work. He hurriedly drove into the parking lot, parked, turned off the windshield wipers, jumped out of his car, slammed the door, and ran for the main entrance. That evening, he could not get the car started. The battery was dead. He got a jump start from a co-worker, drove home, and used his battery recharger to put a good charge on the battery. But despite careful testing, he never found out why the battery went dead. Can you?

Clues: 52/Answer: 226.

SAFE SMASH-UP

A car slowly started to move forward. Then it picked up speed. Faster and faster it went, until it crashed through a guardrail and went over a cliff. It fell over a hundred feet and was very badly damaged. No one was killed or injured. In fact, no one was even afraid of being killed or injured. Why not?

Clues: 44/Answer: 222.

CONTAGIOUS CARSICKNESS?

Stan and Jan were driving along a highway. Fran, a small child strapped into the back seat, said "I feel sick." "It's probably carsickness," replied Jan. "We'll be stopping soon," said Stan, "then you can get out for some fresh air." Less than ten minutes later, Stan shut off the engine and they all got out of the car. But within half an hour, Jan complained: "Fran has motion sickness, and I do, too." Jan did not normally get carsick. What was happening?

Clues: 33/Answer: 216.

THE LATE TRAIN

Amanda got onto a train. After traveling about one thousand miles, she got off. She arrived at her destination forty-five minutes late. There had been no delays, and the train had picked her up on time. Why was it late?

Clues: 38/Answer: 218.

OFFICES ODDITIES

STUBBORN STEVE

Steve went to buy a package of standard-size paper. "We have a special today," a sales clerk told Steve. "It's a better grade of paper, and it's cheaper, too." Steve investigated and found that the paper on sale was the same size and color, but of a heavier weight than the paper he had in his hand. It would be less likely to jam in printers or copiers than the paper he had chosen. And, it *was* much less expensive. Why, therefore, did Steve decline the paper on sale and retain his original choice?

Clues: 48/Answer: 224.

THE NONSTOP ELEVATOR TRIP

Bill got to his appointment on time. "I was worried about those elevators for a minute," said Bill, "but I figured out a way to get here faster." Then he explained his reasoning. "Never thought of that," said Jill, who worked there and greeted him, "but if you just get in an elevator, it sure can take a long time. I have a way to beat the system, too." "What's your way?" he asked. "I just get in, and when the elevator first stops, I get out," she replied. He couldn't figure out how that strategy would save any time. Can you?

Clues: 42/Solution: 221.

MAKING THE GRADE

Nervous Nell, a college student with a straight-A average, went into her professor's office. She told the receptionist she was worried about her grade on the final paper for her course "Is there some way

I can be notified of my final grade as soon as possible?" asked Nell. The receptionist replied, "If you hand in a self-addressed stamped postcard with your term paper, the professor will write the grade on it and mail it to you as soon as the paper is graded. That's much faster than waiting for a transcript." "Oh," said Nell, "but I don't think I can do that." Why not?

Clues: 40/Answer: 219.

A MYSTERY FAX

When his private phone line rang and he picked it up, the business executive heard a loud, squealing noise. Why did he receive a fax call on his private line, a phone that was well known not to have a fax machine connected to it?

Clues: 41/Answer: 220.

THE FAST ELEVATOR TRIP

Bill was nearly late for an appointment in a tall office building. He ran into the building, reached the elevators that led to the correct range of floors, pressed the button, and waited. After a tense few minutes, an elevator arrived and opened its doors to receive passengers. Why didn't he get on?

Clues: 35/Answer: 217.

ASININE ACTIONS

GIVING WAYNE THE BOOT

Wayne was asleep when a boot crashed through his bedroom window, waking him up. Loud music came from the house next door, further irritating him. He jumped up, shook his fist at his neighbor's house, and shouted some obscenities toward it. "It's three a.m.," he yelled truthfully. "If you don't turn down that racket now, I'm calling the cops!" The music persisted, and Wayne did as he had threatened and called the police. When they arrived, the officers refused to prosecute for the noise, even though it was obviously excessively loud. After the police officers explained the facts to Wayne, he was happy to forgive not only the noise, but also the broken window. Explain.

Clues: 36/Answer: 217.

RACING THE DRAWBRIDGE

Park Street included a drawbridge over a river. As its warning lights flashed, Clarence proceeded toward the bridge. The barriers were lowered, blocking the road. Clarence ignored them. The drawbridge itself opened, and Clarence gunned the motor and aimed right at it. But there was no collision. Why not?

Clues: 44/Answer: 221.

SCARED OF HER SHADOW?

Wacky Wendy, who lives in Florida, finds it particularly important, when she is driving and sees the shadow of her car, to roll down her window. Why?

Clues: 44/Answer: 222.

PICTURE THE TOURISTS

"I have a manual focus camera," said Sherman Shutterbug to his friend Sal as they sat next to each other on a tour bus. "Mine is autofocus," replied Sal. "It's much quicker because the camera measures the distance to whatever I'm photographing and focuses automatically." "Then I think we'd better change places," said Sherman. Why?

Clues: 43/Answer: 221.

THE MIRROR

A mirror is mounted over the headboard of a bed. It is there because someone has a bad back. Explain.

Clues: 40/Answer: 220.

THE EMPTY WRAPPER

A woman was at the checkout lane of a supermarket. She removed several items from her cart and put them on the conveyor belt that led to the cashier. The cashier noted their prices and passed the items along to be bagged. A perfectly ordinary process, but one of the items entered and passed along was an empty wrapper. The cashier realized that the wrapper was empty, but charged her for it anyway. Why?

Clues: 35/Answer: 216.

SECRET FUEL

Marvin often sneaked into his neighbor's driveway in the middle of the night in the course of playing a prank. He would quietly unscrew the fuel cap from his neighbor's car and pour gasoline into its fuel tank. What was he up to?

Clues: 45/Answer: 222.

FORGOT TO STOP?

Angus was driving along a road at about thirty miles per hour. Suddenly, he jumped out of his car. He had not applied the brakes, and the car was still moving. He was not a stunt man for a movie or otherwise involved in deliberately risky activity. What happened?

Clues: 35/Answer: 217.

SHORT-LIVED MESSAGES

Yolanda regularly writes and destroys messages to herself. Usually, people write such notes as reminders, such as in calendars. But Yolanda never expects to forget what was in the messages. Why write them?

Clues: 46/Answer: 223.

MORE SHORT-LIVED WRITING

Yolanda often passes a writing instrument across a surface for which it is intended and, within a few seconds, erases the result. What is she doing?

Clues: 41/Answer: 220.

I'VE GOT YOUR NUMBER

Kingfist, a bookie well known for aggressive collection practices, was pursuing Sam Skiptown, who owed him money. From a distance, he spotted Sam and quietly followed him to his house. The house was well guarded, with a burglar alarm system and a climbable but inconvenient fence. Kingfist made plans. Within a week, he called Sam and warned him: "Pay now, or take the consequences." Sam was horrified. "How did you get my number?" he asked. "No questions," ordered Kingfist. "Let's just say I went to a lot of trouble to ask you nicely." Sam never figured out how Kingfist learned his telephone number, which was unpublished and known to only a few trusted friends. Can you?

Clues: 37/Answer: 218.

HAPHAZARD HAPPENINGS

THE MAIL IS IN!

One day earlier, little Oscar had mailed in an order form for a wanted toy. Now, he was constantly pestering his mother to let him check the mail. Suddenly, while looking out the window at the apartment complex mailboxes, he shouted, "The mail is in! The mail is in!" Neither he nor his mother had seen a mail carrier, mail truck, or any activity near the mailboxes, but Oscar was right; it was in. How had he known?

Clues: 40/Answer: 219.

MAGAZINE SUBSCRIPTIONS

Magazines often contain postcards meant for use by new subscribers. Some people consider them a nuisance and just toss them out. Some don't, even though they won't ever use them for their intended purpose. Why not throw them away?

Clues: 39/Answer: 219.

SOLICITING IN SEATTLE

Two friends, who lived in different well-to-do neighborhoods in Seattle, were conversing. "Almost every week, I get a few people who knock on my door and ask for money," said one. "Odd. That rarely happens to me," replied the other. But there is a good explanation for the difference. What is it?

Clues: 47/Answer: 223.

NOT FROM THE USA

Belinda Blabbermouth told a riddle. "I am standing in a place where I can travel north, south, east, or west, and soon be in the USA. Where am I?" After everyone gave up, she laughed, "The USA, of course!" After a few seconds, someone else spoke up: "Not necessarily. The country I come from, for example." Where was he from?

Clues: 42/Answer: 221.

DOTS ON THE I'S

"The teacher marked you wro-ong," Jimmy sang out teasingly during school recess. "You didn't put dots on all your I's!" "Is that so!" countered Timmy. "Betcha don't know how to draw a small I with a dot on it!" he challenged. Jimmy did so, and Timmy looked defeated. A few moments later, Timmy retorted, "Well, now I have dots over my I's and you don't!" One glance at Timmy and Jimmy burst out laughing. So did Timmy. Half the class did, too. Explain.

Clues: 33/Answer: 216.

POWER FAILURE

While Horace slept peacefully, a transformer on the street burned out and stopped all electrical power to his house. The power was restored two hours later, while Horace was still asleep. He awoke the next morning and noted with annoyance that all of his digital clocks were blinking and had to be reset. "I hate power failures," he grumbled, as he carried his battery-powered watch to the VCR, the microwave oven, and other devices that needed to have their clocks reset. But Horace had no idea that the power had failed during the night, much less how long. Explain.

Clues: 43/Answer: 221.

LONG-LIFE BULBS

Eccentric Eric flipped an ordinary light switch in his living room. The lights went on, apparently in an ordinary way. But there was special hidden circuitry involved. He was right when he boasted, "My lights are wired so the bulbs last much longer than average. I rarely have to change them." Explain.

Clues: 39/Answer: 219.

THEY HAD A BALL

Two men stood on a softball field and practiced throwing and catching just before a game. "Over here! Over here!" shouted Ned, slapping his fist into his mitt. Ted threw the softball to him. "Good catch! Throw me a grounder!" shouted Ted. Ned returned the ball by throwing it along the ground, as requested. "Now a high one! Right here! Right here!" Ted threw the ball high in the air—and Ned ran about ten feet to his left, reached up, and caught the ball easily. "Good arm, but your aim is a little crooked," he announced. "No it isn't," replied Ted." "So what's wrong with throwing the high ball right to where I was standing?" retorted Ned. What indeed?

Clues: 49/Answer: 224.

ECCENTRIC ELECTRONICS

HAPPY WITH THE TV AD

A man went to a TV station and bought one minute's worth of advertising time. He handed a videocassette to the station manager and learned to the second exactly when his one-minute tape

would be on the station. Just before the scheduled time, the man turned on his TV set, tuned it to the correct channel, and waited. At exactly the time for his ad, a test pattern came on. The sound, an intense pure tone, did not change for a full minute. The picture stayed the same, too. Then the man, pleased, turned off his TV set. Explain.

Clues: 37/Annswer: 217.

TIME FOR REPAIRS

Dilton got a new digital watch and put it on his wrist. At work, he looked at the office clock and checked his watch. They showed the same time. Later that morning, he couldn't make sense of what his watch showed and decided to return it to the store. Then, before lunch, he again noted that his watch showed the correct time. During his lunch break, he returned to the store. But the salesclerk to whom he showed the watch noted that it showed the correct time, and Dilton agreed that it did. Dilton was soon satisfied that he had a watch that worked perfectly. But the clerk neither opened it for repairs nor replaced it. Explain.

Clues: 49/Answer: 225.

WATCHING THE GAME

Elmer had a sports bar, one with several TV screens hooked up to a satellite receiver and tuned to receive popular sports events. One day, there was a ball game in a stadium nearby. The game was blacked out from the local TV stations and even from local satellite receivers, but Elmer and his customers saw the game on TV anyway. How?

Clues: 51/Answer: 225.

STRANGE SOUNDS

Modern movies, unlike those of half a century ago, are often made with picture and sound recorded at different times. Sound-effects technicians watch the picture and make the appropriate

sounds, perhaps walking in place on a hard floor to generate the sound of footsteps. How can this method of recording sound be detected in the final movies

Clues: 48/Answer: 224.

THE TV OBEYED

Jake had some friends over to watch a popular new movie on his brand-new big-screen TV with state-of-the-art surround-sound loudspeakers. As the credits ended and everyone went to the kitchen for snacks, an obnoxious commercial came on. Jake turned to the set. "Oh, shut up!" he shouted angrily at the TV—and it did! Explain what happened.

Clues: 50/Answer: 225.

NO TV TROUBLE

Stuart was driving a car along a highway. A small TV set sat on the dashboard, and Stuart could see its screen. The theme music from Stuart's favorite TV show came on. At a police roadblock set up to screen and catch lawbreakers, a state trooper observed Stuart and his TV set, but did not warn or arrest him. Why not?

Clues: 42/Answer: 220.

INEFFICIENCY PAYS OFF

A certain mechanical object is often made in several models by each of its manufacturers. Government regulations require that its retail sellers offer information that will allow part of the cost of operation to be calculated. From each manufacturer, the models of the object offered can be ranked from least to most expensive. The cheapest model costs relatively little to buy and operate and has simple controls. The most expensive model costs most to operate and generally has the most elaborate controls. But the most expensive model is not necessarily the most effective at doing what it is designed to do. What is the object?

Clues: 38/Answer: 218.

MONEY MADNESS

SECRET BUSINESS

Two men were on the telephone, discussing a multimillion-dollar business deal. They used electronic scramblers so that no one could easily listen in on their conversation. They also each had much more sophisticated scramblers, which were harder to obtain and which encoded conversations more securely than the scramblers that they used. Why did they use the less secure scramblers?

Clues: 45/Answer: 222.

YOUTHFUL GAMBLE

Some people gamble irrationally and are at risk of losing more money than they can afford to. Laws exist, therefore, to prohibit gambling except under special circumstances. It would seem especially important to keep young adults from gambling, for bad habits can be formed while young that cannot be easily corrected later. But certain young adults are allowed to gamble, in that they pay money and receive something of greater or lesser value in exchange for that money, which is partially determined by chance. Explain.

Clues: 52/Answer: 226.

EASY MONEY

The TV set had a retail value of $100. Butch worked at the whole-sale warehouse and said that stores bought them for $60 each. The warehouse bought them in large lots for $45 apiece. He offered to sell you all you want for $30 each. If they cost $45, then how could he make a profit at $30?   *Clues: 34/Answer: 216.*

GAS-STATION GLITCH

During a fuel shortage, George drove to a gas station and waited in line behind many other motorists. A man in the familiar gas-station uniform walked over and explained to him, "We have a ten-dollar limit. To save time, we are taking cash only and collecting payment in advance." George gave the man a ten-dollar bill. When he reached the front of the line and parked in front of a pump, he asked for his ten dollars' worth of gas. "The limit is five dollars," replied the attendant. What happened?   *Clues: 36/Answer: 217.*

STAGED ROULETTE

Police officers, their spouses, and their families put together a talent show to raise money for their retirement fund. One of the events at the show was a skit about the evils of gambling. In one scene, a mis-guided man lost most of his money to a crooked roulette-wheel operator. It was learned too late that the audience could see the stage from above and would observe the number into which a roulette ball would drop. What did the producers do?

Clues: 47/Answer: 224.

CLUES TO CLEVER PUZZLES

∿ Arrested Anyway

Q: Was Rocky wanted for a previous crime?

A: No.

Q: Did Rocky have to change planes?

A: Yes.

Q: When Rocky checked his suitcase, did he expect it to be delivered directly to his final destination?

A: No.

∿ Burning Down the Building

Q: Did anyone bribe the landlord?

A: No.

Q: Did the fire destroy evidence of a crime?

A: No.

Q: Did a tenant set the fire, perhaps out of anger?

A: No.

∾ **Caught in the Act**

Q: Was he really a pickpocket?

A: Yes.

Q: Did he want to be arrested?

A: No.

Q: Did he act rationally?

A: Yes.

∾ **Contagious Carsickness?**

Q: Was there something wrong with the car?

A: No.

Q: When Jan felt sick, were they all breathing fresh air?

A: Yes.

Q: Were they then outside the car?

A: Yes.

∾ **Dots on the I's**

Q: Is a small I with a dot over it commonly seen?

A: No.

Q: If Timmy had written his statement, instead of spoken it, then would the puzzle be easy?

A: Yes.

Q: In his retort, was Timmy talking about the same thing that Jimmy had teased him about earlier?

A: No.

∿ Driving the Wrong Car

Q: Did each car have a hitch and compatible bumper, allowing either car to tow the other awhile if both worked?

A: Yes.

Q: Was the broken car smashed so it would not tow easily?

A: No.

Q: Was the only problem with the broken car related to its brakes, so the other car could be towed with its brakes partially set?

A: No.

∿ Easy Money

Q: Would Butch keep his word and deliver one complete and working TV set for each $30 you paid him?

A: Yes.

Q: Did he obtain the set from the inventory that had cost his employer $45 each?

A: Yes.

Q: Did Butch lose money on the transaction?

A: No.

∿ The Empty Wrapper

Q: Was the incident an attempt to cheat the customer, or related to fraud in any context?

A: No.

Q: Did the woman who removed the wrapper from the cart know that the wrapper was empty?

A: Yes.

Q: Was the woman accompanied while she shopped?

A: Yes.

∿ The Fast Elevator Trip

Q: Was the elevator working properly and able to go to the floor where Bill had his appointment?

A: Yes.

Q: Was Bill prevented from getting on, as by a work crew loading a piece of heavy machinery?

A: No.

Q: Did Bill correctly reason that he would get to his appointment faster by not using that elevator?

A: Yes.

∿ Forgot to Stop?

Q: One minute before Angus jumped out of the car, did he expect to do so?

A: No.

Q: After he jumped out of the car, did he expect to get into it again?

A: No.

Q: Did more than two minutes pass between when Angus jumped out of the car and when he reached the ground?

A: Yes.

∾ Gas-Station Glitch

Q: Was the attendant who announced the five-dollar limit telling the truth?

A: Yes.

Q: Did George, after receiving fuel, receive five dollars in change from the attendant?

A: No.

Q: Was George likely to be one of several angry customers at the gas station?

A: Yes.

∾ Giving Wayne the Boot

Q: Were the police officers honest and Wayne's neighbor not politically influential?

A: Yes.

Q: Was it the same person who turned on the loud music and threw the boot through Wayne's window?

A: Yes.

Q: Was the neighbor happy when the police arrived?

A: Yes.

∿ Happy with the TV Ad

Q: Had an accomplice damaged the TV station, its transmitter, or anything related to it?

A: No.

Q: Did the man hope to sell diagnostic TV repair services or TV sets?

A: No.

Q: Would he have been pleased if the test pattern had appeared at a different time or on another channel?

A: No.

∿ He Called the Police

Q: Did he call a co-conspirator on the police force?

A: No.

Q: Before breaking in, had he intended to call the police?

A: No.

Q: Was he arrested?

A: Yes.

∿ I've Got Your Number

Q: Did Kingfist obtain the telephone number from confederates at the phone company or from Sam's friends?

A: No.

Q: Did he enter the house?

A: No.

Q: Is the fact that Sam's fence was climbable significant?

A: Yes.

∾ Inefficiency Pays Off

Q: Does the difference in effectiveness relate to reliability or to relative availability of parts in case of a breakdown?

A: No.

Q: Is an expensive model of the object significantly more likely to be stolen than a cheaper one, making the cheaper one preferable in high-crime areas?

A: No.

Q: Can the elaborate controls be more easily misused than the simple ones?

A: No.

∾ The Late Train

Q: Does the lateness have anything to do with the train's having crossed from one time zone to another?

A: No.

Q: At the time Amanda stepped onto the train, did its crew expect it to become late before she got off it?

A: Yes.

Q: Could this incident, for this reason, happen only at a particular time of year?

A: Yes.

∾ Long-Life Bulbs

Q: Were the bulbs totally ordinary?

A: Yes.

Q: The ordinary incandescent bulbs screwed into ordinary sockets, but could a fluorescent bulb that had a socket base and that fit into the fixtures be used instead?

A: No.

Q: Does the answer have to do with the structure of incandescent bulbs?

A: Yes.

∾ Magazine Subscriptions

Q: Could the need anticipated by those who save them be satisfied by blank paper of similar size and shape?

A: No.

Q: Are they used to cause troublesome paperwork by writing someone else's name on them and then mailing them?

A: No.

Q: Is their reply-paid status very important, more so than for an ordinary postcard?

A: Yes.

∾ **The Mail Is In!**

Q: Had Oscar put the order form into the outgoing mail slot next to the mailboxes the previous day, after that day's mail had been delivered?

A: Yes.

Q: Did the mailboxes have big pods nearby so that a mail carrier could put a parcel in one of them and the key to that pod in that resident's mailbox?

A: Yes.

Q: Did Oscar pay particular attention to the pods?

A: Yes.

∾ **Making the Grade**

Q: Did Nell want a good grade on the course, so that she was planning to have her paper properly written and handed in on or before the deadline?

A: Yes.

Q: Did she have any reason to doubt the receptionist?

A: No.

Q: Is her straight-A average, which suggests good study habits, significant?

A: Yes.

∾ **The Mirror**

Q: Is the mirror where anyone could easily look directly into it?

A: No.

Q: Is it made from ordinary plate glass?

A: No.

Q: Is it the only mirror that is mounted near the bed?

A: No.

∾ More Short-Lived Writing

Q: Are computers or any other electronic devices involved?

A: No.

Q: By what she is doing, does she intend to communicate to anyone?

A: No.

Q: Although it is immediately erased, does her output from the writing instrument in turn help erase something else?

A: Yes.

∾ A Mystery Fax

Q: Was the call a wrong or misdialed number?

A: No.

Q: If the executive had anticipated the call and connected a fax machine to his telephone line, then would the fax call have resulted in his receiving a fax transmission?

A: No.

Q: Did the executive know who or what originated the fax call?

A: Yes.

∾ No TV Trouble

Q: Is it legal for a TV set to be operated so that the driver of a moving motor vehicle can see its screen?

A: No.

Q: Did Stuart know the state trooper, bribe him, or have any special influence?

A: No.

Q: Did Stuart hear the theme music in stereo?

A: Yes.

∾ The Nonstop Elevator Trip

Q: Were they on a high floor in an office building?

A: Yes.

Q: Did the building have separate groups of elevators to serve separate ranges of floors?

A: Yes.

Q: Could anyone get into a crowded elevator on the ground floor and reasonably expect to get directly to the floor where Bill was, without having the elevator stop at other floors first?

A: No.

∾ Not from the USA

Q: He was not from the USA, but would he necessarily speak English with a recognizably foreign accent?

A: No.

Q: Was he referring to dry non-USA land, and not an island?

A: Yes.

Q: Could the USA be reached by traveling less than 150 miles north, south, east, or west from one point in his home country?

A: Yes.

∾ Picture the Tourists

Q: Did Sherman want to change places so that he would get better pictures for himself?

A: No.

Q: Was Sherman originally sitting next to a window?

A: Yes.

Q: Was the window open?

A: No.

∾ Power Failure

Q: Did Horace sleep away from his house and return to it to find the clocks all stopped?

A: No.

Q: Was he of sound mind and with good vision?

A: Yes.

Q: Did he own an electric clock that had an hour hand and a minute hand?

A: No.

∾ Racing the Drawbridge

Q: Was Clarence sensible?

A: Yes.

Q: Did he turn away or stop?

A: No.

Q: If the drawbridge was closed, then would Clarence have approached the bridge?

A: No.

∾ Safe Smash-Up

Q: Was the car controlled by a radio-operated device, as for a movie?

A: No.

Q: Was the car deliberately damaged?

A: No.

Q: Did the car catch fire after its fuel line burst?

A: No.

∾ Scared of Her Shadow?

Q: Does the sun shine brightly in Florida?

A: Yes.

Q: Is the reason for opening a car window concerned with controlling the temperature in the car?

A: No.

Q: When the sun is shining brightly behind a car, which is not the same as shining in a driver's eyes, is there potential danger because something important cannot be seen?

A: Yes.

∾ Secret Business

Q: Did they use scramblers because they suspected that their telephones were tapped?

A: Yes.

Q: In this particular context, would the secure scramblers, which were compatible with each other, have been as useful as the ones that they actually used?

A: No.

Q: Did the men discuss all of their plans on the telephone?

A: No.

∾ Secret Fuel

Q: Was the gasoline adulterated, the wrong octane rating, or otherwise intended to make the car run poorly?

A: No.

Q: Did the neighbor know of Marvin's activities?

A: No.

Q: Was the car covered by a warranty?

A: Yes.

∿ She Arrived On Time

Q: Could Carol have driven from home to the coffee house in two minutes, at less than a hundred miles per hour?

A: No.

Q: Did she use unusual transportation, such as a helicopter?

A: No.

Q: Did Daryl dial her home number correctly and reach her by doing so?

∿ Short-Lived Messages

Q: Does she show them to someone else, perhaps because they are cue cards for a newscaster?

A: No.

Q: Are the messages intermediate steps in mathematical calculations or part of the process of encoding secret data?

A: No.

Q: Are they intermediate steps in an electronic message-handling process that is familiar to the public?

A: Yes.

∾ Smashed Taillights

Q: Did the owner give Bob permission to smash the taillights?

A: No.

Q: Had the car been stolen?

A: No.

Q: After the taillights were smashed, was something important revealed behind them?

A: Yes.

∾ Soliciting in Seattle

Q: Do the two friends have similar age and ethnicity, live in similar single-family houses, and live in neighborhoods that, though not close to each other, have virtually identical demographic statistics?

A: Yes.

Q: Is the explanation related to an anti-canvassing ordinance that affects one neighborhood but not the other?

A: No.

Q: Can the difference be traced to the personal convenience of the canvassers?

A: Yes.

∾ Staged Roulette

Q: Could the skit be rewritten so that the roulette bet was concealed from the view of the audience, or removed entirely?

A: No.

Q: Could the roulette wheel be partially hidden?

A: No.

Q: Was gambling a significant problem in that town?

Q: Yes

∿ Strange Sounds

Q: Are the sounds and pictures out of sync, as when words on a foreign-language film don't match the speaker's lips?

A: No.

Q: Do mistimed sounds—too early or late—give it away?

A: No.

Q: Are some sounds inappropriately absent?

A: Yes.

∿ Stubborn Steve

Q: Did Steve choose paper that was multiple-part, tractor-feed, or otherwise special or unusual?

A: No.

Q: Was the sales clerk completely honest and accurate?

A: Yes.

Q: Was the paper intended for an exotic use that was not reasonably expected by its manufacturer, such as papiermâché or analysis under a microscope?

A: No.

∾ Supposed to Kill?

Q: Did the intended victim run or call for help?

A: No.

Q: Having learned that the gun was not loaded, did anyone try to grab it or otherwise forcibly intervene?

A: No.

Q: The incident did not result in death or serious injury. Did anyone want it to?

A: No.

∾ They Had a Ball

Q: Did Ted intend to give Ned practice at running to catch a high ball?

A: No.

Q: Could Ted have aimed the ball directly at Ned if he had wanted to?

A: Yes.

Q: Is their location significant?

A: Yes.

∾ Time for Repairs

Q: Did the watch work properly, even though Dilton at first didn't think it did?

A: Yes.

Q: Earlier, had Dilton properly set it to the correct time?

A: Yes.

Q: When Dilton noticed something wrong, was the watch showing an incorrect time from running too fast or slow?

A: No.

∿ A Token Wait in a Token Line

Q: Did Smart Stephanie have someone buy her tokens, or go to the subway station at odd, "off-peak" hours?

A: No.

Q: Did she sneak under turnstiles, otherwise evade the fare, or have permission to use the subway without paying (as can some police officers, subway employees, and such)?

A: No.

Q: Did she live in a strictly residential district and work in a strictly business district during ordinary business hours?

A: Yes.

∿ The TV Obeyed

Q: Did Jake shout to operate a sound-sensitive switch or, while shouting, manually operate a remote-control device or an ordinary switch?

A: No.

Q: Did Jake see the TV screen just before he shouted?

A: Yes.

Q: Videotaped movies usually have their durations printed on their boxes. Is that fact significant?

A: Yes.

∿ Watching the Game

Q: Did Elmer use an illegally manufactured descrambler?

A: No.

Q: Did he have an accomplice at a TV station or at a satellite company?

A: No.

Q: Did he have a noncompeting accomplice who ran another sports bar?

A: Yes.

∿ Welcome, Slasher

Q: Were the boy and the policeman what they appeared to be and not, for example, actors for a movie?

A: Yes.

Q: Was the policeman honest?

A: Yes.

Q: Did the boy act in retaliation, perhaps to deter a criminal who could not be prosecuted by normal methods?

A: No.

∾ **What Drained the Battery?**

Q: When Walter returned to the car, was anything switched on or the hood open?

A: No.

Q: Had anyone been in the parking lot since Walter parked his car and ran inside?

A: Yes.

Q: Did Walter lock his car?

A: No.

∾ **Youthful Gamble**

Q: Is the gambling sometimes managed or controlled by a state government or one of its agencies?

A: Yes.

Q: Are certain young adults not only permitted but also required to gamble?

A: Yes.

Q: Can the gambling be repeated by putting one's winnings at financial risk?

A: No.

∾∾∾

TRICKY PUZZLES

PRETTY TRICKY

THE TRACKS OF MY TIRES

The police found a murder victim and they noticed a pair of tire tracks leading to and from the body. They followed the tracks to a nearby farmhouse where two men and a woman were sitting on the porch. There was no car at the farmhouse and none of the three could drive. The police arrested the woman. Why?

Clues: 103/Answer: 238.

THE UPSET WOMAN

When the woman saw him she was upset. Even though she had never seen him before, she had left some food for him because she knew he would be hungry. But he could not reach the food because he had an iron bar across his back. He died soon after and the woman was pleased. What's going on?

Clues: 105/Answer: 239.

BERTHA'S TRAVELS

Every day Bertha travels thirty miles in the course of her work. She doesn't travel in a wheeled vehicle and never has problems with traffic, the police, weather, or airports. What does she do?

Clues: 86/Answer: 227.

SICK LEAVE

Walter spent three days in the hospital. He was neither sick nor injured, but when it was time to leave he had to be carried out. Why?

Clues: 100/Answer: 236.

TOP AT LAST

William was the least intelligent and laziest boy in a class of thirty students who took an examination. Yet, when the results were announced, William's name was at the top of the list. Why?

Clues: 103/Answer: 238.

CRIMINAL ASSISTANCE

The police put up notices warning the public about a certain type of crime, but this actually helped the criminals. How?

Clues: 88/Answer: 228.

IN THE MIDDLE OF THE NIGHT

A man wakes up at night in the pitch dark. He knows that on his bedside table are a razor, a watch, and a glass of water. How can he reach out onto the table and be sure to pick up the watch without touching either the razor or the glass of water?

Clues: 93/Answer: 232.

HONORABLE INTENT

Six people who do not know each other get together to honor a seventh person unknown to all of them. Why?

Clues: 92/Answer: 231.

SHELL SHOCK

Why do players very rarely win at the "shell game," where they have to say which of three shuffled shells covers a pea?

Clues: 99/Answer: 236.

WONDERFUL WEATHER

A ship sank in perfect weather conditions. If the weather had been worse, the ship would probably not have sunk. What happened?

Clues: 105/Answer: 240.

MATERIAL WITNESS

In the fabric shop, the curtains are neatly arranged by style. The floral-patterned ones are in a section marked "Floral," the plain ones are in a section marked "Plain," and the striped ones are in a section marked "Striped." But one pair with vertical blue stripes is not in the "Striped" section. Why not?

Clues: 95/Answer: 233.

DENISE AND HARRY

Denise died at sea while Harry died on land. People were pleased that Harry had died and even more pleased that Denise had died. Why was that?

Clues: 89/Answer: 229.

MECHANICAL ADVANTAGE

A driver had a problem with his car in a remote area miles from the nearest garage. He stopped at a little candy store, where his problem was quickly solved. How?

Clues: 95/Answer: 233.

LIFESAVER

A politician made a speech that saved his life even before he gave the speech. How?   *Clues: 94/Answer: 232.*

UNFINISHED BUSINESS

What work can a sculptor never finish?

Clues: 104/Answer: 239.

THE DEADLY DRESSER

A healthy man got dressed and then lay down and died. Why?

Clues: 88/Answer: 228.

LANDLUBBER

A man sailed single-handedly around the world in a small boat. Yet he was always in sight of land. How come?

Clues: 93/Answer: 232.

ANOTHER LANDLUBBER

A man went around the world in a ship. Yet he was always in sight of land. Why?

Clues: 86/Answer: 227.

PLANE AND SIMPLE

A boy who is three feet tall puts a nail into a tree at his exact height. He returns two years later when he has grown by six inches and the tree has grown by twelve inches. How much taller is the nail than the boy?

Clues: 97/Answer: 234.

JERICHO

A man was building a house when it collapsed all around him. He wasn't injured or upset, and he calmly started to rebuild it. What was going on? *Clues: 93/Answer: 232.*

SUPERIOR KNOWLEDGE

When the mother superior returned to the convent after a weekend away, she immediately noticed that a man had been there— and that was strictly against the rules. How did she know?

Clues: 102/Answer: 238.

HALF FOR ME AND HALF FOR YOU

It has been said that Lucrezia Borgia once split an apple in half and shared it with a companion. Within 10 minutes her companion was dead and Lucrezia survived. Why?

Clues: 91/Answer: 231.

RUSH JOB

In 1849, a man went to the California gold rush hoping to make his fortune by selling tents to the miners. However, the weather was fine and the miners slept out in the open, so the man could sell no tents. But he made his fortune anyway and his name is famous to this day. How did he become rich and who is he?

Clues: 99/Answer: 236.

THE ENGRAVING

A woman saw an advertisement for a color engraving of Queen Elizabeth II for $1 and bought it. When it arrived, she had no cause for complaint, but she wasn't pleased. Why?

Clues: 90/Answer: 229.

WHO DID IT?

A child at school printed something rude on the wall and nobody owned up to doing it. How did the teacher find out who did it?

Clues: 105/Answer: 240.

LETHAL RELIEF

A famine-stricken Third World country was receiving food aid from the West, but this inadvertently led to the deaths of several people. How?

Clues: 94/Answer: 232.

HOT JOB

A man held up a bank on a hot day. He was caught later by the police. On a colder day he would probably not have been caught. Why?   *Clues: 92/Answer: 231.*

CHOP CHOP

Why was an ancient, rare, and healthy tree that stood well away from all buildings in the grounds of Cork University condemned to be cut down?

Clues: 87/Answer: 227.

WALLY TEST I

From the World Association of Learning, Laughter, and Youth (WALLY) comes the WALLY Test! It is a set of very rapid-fire questions that may look easy, but be warned—they are designed to trick you. Write down your answers on a piece of paper, and then see how many you got right. The time limit is three minutes.

1. If a man bets you that he can bite his eye, should you take the bet?

2. If he now bets you that he can bite his other eye, should you take that bet?

3. How can you stand behind someone while he or she stands behind you?

4. What looks like a horse, moves likes a horse, and is as big as a horse but weighs nothing?

5. Who is bigger: Mr. Bigger or Mr. Bigger's son?

6. Tom's mother had three children. One was named April. One was named May. What was the third one named?

7. Where could you go to see an ancient pyramid, an iceberg, and a huge waterfall?

8. What has four fingers and a thumb but isn't a hand?

9. What multiplies by division?

10. What's white when it's dirty, and black when it's clean?

Answers on page 241.

AWFULLY TRICKY

FOREIGN CURE

Why does an American fly to another country in the hope of finding a cure for his illness?

Clues: 90/Answer: 230.

SPIES ARE US

During World War I, two German spies often ate at the same restaurant, but they never sat together. How did they pass information?

Clues: 101/Answer: 237.

TITTLE TATTLE

You have seen many tittles in the last few minutes. What are they?

Clues: 102/Answer: 238.

OUTSTANDING

What feature of *The Old Farmer's Almanac* made it vastly more popular than all its rivals for over 100 years in the rural U.S.?

Clues: 97/Answer: 234.

THE STUFFED CLOUD

A meteorologist was replaced in his job because of a stuffed cloud. What's a stuffed cloud?

Clues: 102/Answer: 237.

A STRANGE COLLECTION

At a dinner, a small container is passed around the table and every guest puts something in it. The contents are then thrown away. What's going on?

Clues: 101/Answer: 237.

BUS-LANE BONUS

A city introduced bus lanes on busy streets and the death rate dropped quickly. Why?

Clues: 86/Answer: 227.

BLOW BY BLOW

Why was a man at a fairground blowing darts through a concealed blowpipe?

Clues: 86/Answer: 227.

HISTORY QUESTION

What happened in London on September 8, 1752?

Clues: 92/Answer: 231.

SIGN HERE

A man bought two identical signs but found that he could use only one of them. Why?

Clues: 100/Answer: 236.

PAPER TIGER

A man writes the same number, and nothing else, on twenty sheets of paper. Why?

Clues: 97/Answer: 234.

FORGING AHEAD

A forger went into a store with a genuine $50 bill. How did he use this to come out with a $20 profit?

Clues: 91/Answer: 230.

SMILE, PLEASE !

A man wrote to a toothpaste company suggesting a way in which they could significantly increase their sales. How?

Clues: 101/Answer: 237.

HIGH ON A HILL

A man was marooned overnight on a mountain above the snow line in winter. He had no protective clothing and no tent. How did he survive?

Clues: 92/Answer: 231.

MINE SHAFTED

In order to sell it, a con man salted a useless mine with a number of genuine pieces of silver. How did the buyer figure out the scheme?

Clues: 95/Answer: 233.

RUNNING ON EMPTY

Mrs. Jones was very pleased that the car ran out of gas. Why?

Clues: 99/Answer: 235.

WHAT'S THE POINT?

Why does a woman always use a square pencil in the course of her work?

Clues: 105/Answer: 240.

THE OFFICE JOB

A man applied for a job in an office. When he arrived at the busy, noisy office he was told by the receptionist to fill out a form and wait until he was called. He completed the form and then sat and waited along with four other candidates who had arrived earlier. After a few minutes, he got up and went into an inner office and was subsequently given the job. The other candidates who had arrived earlier were angry. The manager explained why the man had been given the job. What was the reason?

Clues: 96/Answer: 234.

HEARTY APPETITE

A whale ate normally and many people were very disappointed. Why?

Clues: 91/Answer: 231.

THE UPSET BIRD-WATCHER

A keen ornithologist saw a rare bird that he had never seen before, except in illustrations. However, he was very upset. Then he was frightened. Why?

Clues: 104/Answer: 239.

FLOATING HOME

A man went on a long trip and was gone several weeks. When he returned, he was found floating at sea. How come?

Clues: 90/Answer: 230.

CO-LATERAL DAMAGE

During World War II, U.S. forces lost many bombers in raids over Germany due to antiaircraft fire. From the damage on returning bombers, they were able to build up a clear picture of which parts of the planes were hit most frequently and which weren't hit at all. How did they use this information to reduce losses?

Clues: 87/Answer: 228.

ORSON CART

When Orson Welles caused nationwide panic with his radio broadcast of the Martian landing, there was one group that wasn't fooled. Who were they?

Clues: 97/Answer: 234.

THROWING HIS WEIGHT ABOUT

Why did a man who was not suicidal and not threatened in any way throw himself through a plate-glass window on the twentyfourth floor of an office building and so fall to his death?

Clues: 102/Answer: 238.

DISCONNECTED ?

A horse walked all day. Two of its legs traveled twenty-one miles and two legs traveled twenty miles. How come?

Clues: 89/Answer: 229.

JOKER

Four people were playing cards. One played a card and another player immediately jumped up and started to take her clothes off. Why?

Clues: 93/Answer: 232.

RICH MAN, POOR MAN

In England, why did rich people pour their tea first and then add milk while poor people poured milk first and then added tea?

Clues: 98/Answer: 235.

MINED OVER MATTER

A sailor at the bow of his ship saw a mine floating in the water directly in the path of the vessel. There was no time to change the ship's direction. How did he avert disaster?

Clues: 95/Answer: 233.

SURPRISE VISIT

A factory manager gets a tip that the company chairman is on his way to pay a surprise visit. The manager orders the staff to clean the factory, clear out all the trash, and hide it away, but the chairman isn't impressed. Why not?

Clues: 102/Answer: 238.

SCHOOL'S OUT

Why does an elderly lady receive a court order to go to school immediately?

Clues: 99/Answer: 236.

THE DEADLY STONE

A man shot himself because he saw a stone with a small drop of blood on it. Why?

Clues: 89/Answer: 229.

THE COSTLY WAVE

A man waved his hands in the air and this action cost him $30,000. Why?

Clues: 88/Answer: 228.

WALLY TEST II

Time for another WALLY Test. The questions may look easy, but be warned—they're designed to trip you up. Write down your answers on a piece of paper, and then see how many you got right. The time limit is three minutes.

1.   What gets higher as it falls?

2.   How do you stop moles from digging in your garden?

3.   Why did the overweight actor fall through the theater floor?

4.   What happened to the man who invented the silent alarm clock?

5.   What's the best known star with a tail?

6.   How did an actor get his name up in lights in every theater in the country?

7.   Where would you find a square ring?

8.   What do you give a bald rabbit?

9.   How do you make a slow horse fast?

10.   Why did Sam wear a pair of pants with three large holes?

Answers on page: 242.

TERRIBLY TRICKY

2020 VISION

A newspaper editor heard a report that 2,020 pigs had been stolen from a farm, so he called the farmer to check the story. The farmer told him the same story, but the editor changed the number for insertion in the news. Why?

Clues: 103/Answer: 238.

THE GAP

A man was writing the word HIM. Why did he deliberately leave a gap between the final two letters so that it looked a little like HI M?

Clues: 91/Answer: 230.

THE DINNER CLUE

A suspect is interrogated for several hours but doesn't crack. He then demands a meal and soon afterward the police charge him with murder. Why?

Clues: 89/Answer: 229.

THE DEADLY OMELET

A man went into a country inn and ordered an omelet for lunch. He was promptly arrested and later executed. Why?

Clues: 88/Answer: 229.

WRONG WAY

Why does a man who wants to catch a bus going from Alewife to Zebedee deliberately catch one going the opposite way—from Zebedee to Alewife?

Clues: 106/Answer: 240.

THE SINGLE WORD

A woman whom I had never met before was introduced to me. I didn't say a word. She told me about herself, but I didn't say a word. She told me many more things about herself, but I didn't say a word. Eventually I said one word and she was very disappointed. What was the word?

Clues: 100/Answer: 237.

THE MAN WHO WOULD NOT READ

A tourist in England was traveling by train. He had a book with him that he wanted to read, but he didn't start it until he got off the train. Why?

Clues: 95/Answer: 233.

TWO PIGS

A farmer has two pigs that are identical twins from the same litter. However, when he sells them he gets 100 times more for one than the other. Why?

Clues: 104/Answer: 239.

EENSY WEENSY SPIDER FARM

In some parts of France there are spider farms. Why would anybody want to farm spiders?

Clues: 89/Answer: 229.

NOT EATING?

A hungry man has food on his plate but doesn't eat it. Why?

Clues: 96/Answer: 234.

FACE-OFF

In World War I, the French and Austrian armies faced each other. Neither side attacked the other nor fired a shot at the other, yet thousands were killed. How?

Clues: 90/Answer: 230.

CHEAP AND CHEERFUL

A man at a party is offered a choice of a certain food—either the expensive fresh variety or the cheaper canned variety. Why does he choose the cheaper canned food?

Clues: 87/Answer: 227.

UP IN SMOKE

A man owned some excellent cigars, which he smoked. As a result of this he gained $10,000 and a prison sentence. How?

Clues: 104/Answer: 239.

SILLY CONE

How did an office manager achieve greater efficiency using cones?

Clues: 100/Answer: 237.

NOT THE FÜHRER

A body that looked very like that of Adolf Hitler was found by advancing Allied troops near Hitler's bunker in Berlin. The face was destroyed. How did the soldiers quickly find out that it wasn't Hitler's body?

Clues: 96/Answer: 234.

VASE AND MEANS

How did the ancient potters discover the ingredient that made perfect china?

Clues: 105/Answer: 240.

MY CONDIMENTS TO THE CHEF

Why did the owner of a café replace all the bottles of condiments on his tables with packets?

Clues: 96/Answer: 233.

THE MAN WHO DID NOT FLY

Why was a fictitious name added to an airline's passenger list?

Clues: 94/Answer: 233.

INHERITANCE

In ancient Ireland, a king had two sons, each of whom wanted to inherit the kingdom. The king decreed that each should be put in a separate rowboat about one mile from shore and told to row in. The first to touch the shore would inherit the kingdom. The elder and stronger son rowed more quickly and was about to touch the shore with the younger son some 20 yards behind him and farther out to sea. How did the younger son inherit the kingdom?

Clues: 93/Answer: 231.

STAMP DEARTH DEATH

A man died because he didn't buy enough stamps. What happened?

Clues: 101/Answer: 237.

ROCK OF AGES

A man suffered a serious injury because he was listening to rock-and-roll music. What happened?

Clues: 98/Answer: 235.

QUO VADIS?

How was an archaeologist in Britain able to deduce that the Romans drove their chariots on the left-hand side of the road?

Clues: 98/Answer: 235.

FROZEN ASSETS

Why did they build a railway line over the ice when the place could be reached by land and they knew the ice would melt anyway?

Clues: 91/Answer: 230.

PORK PUZZLER

Why did a man who didn't like bacon always pack some bacon when he went on a trip, and throw it out when he arrived?

Clues: 97/Answer: 234.

TURNED OFF

A man inadvertently caused all radio station transmissions in the world to cease. How? And who was he?

Clues: 103/Answer: 238.

THE LAST MAIL

A man mailed two letters to the same address at the same time in the same post office. The letters were identical, but the postage on one letter was more than on the other. Why?

Clues: 94/Answer: 232.

SMALL IS NOT BEAUTIFUL

Why were small cars banned in Sweden?

Clues: 100/Answer: 237.

THE DEADLY FEATHER

A man lies dead next to a feather that caused his death. What happened?

Clues: 88/Answer: 228.

THE SEALED ROOM

A perfectly healthy man was trapped in a sealed room. He died, but not from lack of oxygen. What did he die of?

Clues: 99/Answer: 236.

WRITTEN DOWN

A woman is writing in capital letters. She has difficulty writing the letters A, E, F, G, H, and L, but no difficulty with C, K, M, N, V, and W. Why?

Clues: 106/Answer: 240.

PUBLICITY PUZZLER

A man put an ad in the newspaper. As a result of this, he and another man go shopping together twice a year, but have no other contact. Why?

Clues: 98/Answer: 235.

CLUES TO TRICKY PUZZLES

∾ Another Landlubber

He went around quite quickly.

He saw Africa, Asia, Europe, North America, and South America.

He didn't sail the ship.

∾ Bertha's Travels

Bertha is a woman who normally travels with other people.

She doesn't travel by walking or running, nor by plane or boat.

She provides a service to passengers.

∾ Blow by Blow

He was secretly blowing darts at particular targets.

His nefarious actions generated more sales at the fairground.

∾ Bus-Lane Bonus

The bus lanes were introduced because of heavy traffic congestion. Normal traffic was forbidden to use the bus lanes so the buses could move more quickly.

The reduction in death rate wasn't due to
fewer road accidents, fewer pedestrian accidents,
less pollution, or fewer cars in the city.

Accident victims were saved.

❧ Cheap and Cheerful

The fresh food was in perfectly good condition.

The man was normal and didn't have any allergies
or aversions.

The food was salmon.

❧ Chop Chop

The tree was not hazardous, harmful, or threatening
in any way.

The problem does not involve animals, students, seeds,
leaves, roots, or branches.

The problem related to the tree's location.

❧ Co-lateral Damage

Some damage is fatal to a plane and some is not.

The returning planes are not a true sample
of all the planes and all the damage.

U.S. bomber command used the information
about damage on returning planes to strengthen
planes and so reduce losses.

∾ **The Costly Wave**

He wasn't at an auction.

He waved to fans and onlookers.

∾ **Criminal Assistance**

The police notices were to warn people about
    certain types of thieves.

The thieves observed people's reactions to the signs.

∾ **The Deadly Dresser**

If he had not dressed, he would not have died.

He died by accident.

He was poisoned.

∾ **The Deadly Feather**

The man was physically fit and healthy.

The feather had touched him.

He was a circus performer.

∾ **The Deadly Omelet**

He was a wanted man.

The omelet and its ingredients were relevant.

He had not done anything illegal.

This incident happened in France.

∾ **The Deadly Stone**

The blood on the stone was the man's blood. It had been
put there two days before his death.

Nobody else was involved.

He had marked the stone with his blood for a purpose.

∾ **Denise and Harry**

Denise and Harry harmed people.

They weren't humans but they weren't animals either.

∾ **The Dinner Clue**

The police obtained the evidence they needed.

He didn't finish his meal.

∾ **Disconnected?**

The horse was alive throughout and was not exceptional.

The horse was a working horse.

The two legs that traveled farthest were the front
left and back left.

∾ **Eensy Weensy Spider Farm**

It was relevant that the spider farms were in France.

The spiderwebs were used, but not to catch anything.

They are found in wine-growing regions.

∾ The Engraving

What she received wasn't what she expected.

A fine artist had created the picture she received.

The engraving had already been put to use.

∾ Face-off

The soldiers were killed, but not in action,
nor by disease, flood, storm, or fire.

It was during winter.

Some test shots were fired, but the shells fell well away
from the soldiers.

∾ Floating Home

The man was normal, but he had been on an
extraordinary voyage.

He had not set off by sea, but he had always intended
to return in the manner in which he did.

He returned safe and well. He was found by people
who were concerned for his well-being.

∾ Foreign Cure

He didn't go abroad for drugs, medicines, treatments,
or cures that were unavailable in the United States.

His illness was curable given the right motivation.

He went to an Arab country.

∿ Forging Ahead

He used the $50 bill to help pass a forged bill—but not a forged $50 bill.

He bought something he didn't want.

∿ Frozen Assets

The railway was needed temporarily to carry cargo to a certain location.

It was possible to lay tracks over the land to reach the place, but they were unable to do so.

They wanted to supply food and ammunition.

∿ The Gap

He was writing in an unusual way.

The writing was important and would be seen by many people.

He was planning ahead.

∿ Half for Me and Half for You

Lucrezia Borgia's companion died of poisoning.

The apple was taken at random from a bowl of perfectly good apples.

Lucrezia deliberately killed her companion.

∿ Hearty Appetite

The whale was a killer whale.

The whale was at sea.

The people who were disappointed hadn't come to see the whale.

∼ High on a Hill

The man managed to stay warm but he didn't burn anything.

The man was alone. No person or animal helped him to keep warm.

The mountain was dangerous.

∼ History Question

September 8, 1752, was a very unusual day— but there were ten other days like it.

No significant wars, births, deaths, disasters, achievements, or discoveries happened in London that day.

∼ Honorable Intent

The six people had never met the seventh person and never would meet him.

The seventh person wasn't famous, remarkable, or well known.

The six people all owed a great debt to the seventh person— but not a financial debt.

∼ Hot Job

The robber's face was covered, but he was easily identified.

His choice of clothing was poor.

∽ Inheritance

Both sons reached the shore. The younger was judged
to have touched the shore first.

The younger son took drastic action.

∽ In the Middle of the Night

He didn't hear or smell anything that might have
helped him.

The watch wasn't luminous.

None of the objects could be seen in the pitch dark.

∽ Jericho

Although he constructed it with great care,
the man thought that the house might fall down.

He didn't intend that he or anyone else live in the house.

∽ Joker

They weren't playing strip poker and stripping wasn't
a forfeit or penalty involved in the game.

The actual card game isn't relevant.

She took off her clothes to avoid harm.

∽ Landlubber

He circumnavigated the world and crossed every line
of longitude.

There was nothing special about his boat or on his boat.

He sailed his boat around the world but always stayed

within a few miles of shore.

He did it from November to February.

∾ The Last Mail

There was no difference in the contents, envelope, or addressing of the two letters.

They were both sent by the same method—first class.

The same clerk at the same post office handled both letters.

The man weighed the letters and found their weights were identical. He then put stamps on them and took them to the postal clerk, who told him that one of the letters was fine but that the other needed more stamps.

∾ Lethal Relief

They didn't die of hunger, disease, or food poisoning.

The relief was delivered to remote areas.

The people died before they opened the packages of food.

∾ Lifesaver

Any speech of the same length would have had the same effect.

Someone made an attempt on his life.

∾ The Man Who Did Not Fly

The fictitious person did not exist and did not fly.

The police knew about this situation.

Other passengers had been victims of a crime.

∾ The Man Who Would Not Read

Conditions on the train were perfectly suitable for reading.

He was very obedient.

No local resident would have made the same mistake.

∾ Material Witness

They are perfectly normal curtains and not special.

∾ Mechanical Advantage

The problem wasn't with the engine of his car.

It was raining.

He bought something sweet and used that to solve
the problem.

∾ Mined Over Matter

The mine was live and dangerous. It would explode
if it came into contact with metal.

He took some action to deflect the mine from the ship.

He did not touch or defuse the mine.

∾ Mine Shafted

The buyer explored the mine and found the silver,
as was intended.

They were genuine pieces of silver but not the sort you
would find in a silver mine.

She killed her husband to help someone she loved.

My Condiments to the Chef

The owner wasn't trying to save money or be more efficient.

There had been a problem involving the bottles of vinegar.

He was trying to discourage a certain group of customers.

Not Eating?

The hungry man wanted to eat and there was no medical,
religious, or financial reason for him not to eat.

He was physically fit, healthy, and normal.

He was in the same room as his plate, and the plate
had food on it. But he wasn't able to eat it.

Not the Führer

There was no identity tag or personal effects that would
have revealed the man's identity.

There were no distinguishing marks on the man's body.

His clothing gave the clue.

The Office Job

The man's age, appearance, gender, and dress didn't matter.

Everyone had completed the form correctly
and in a similar fashion.

The man showed that he had a skill required for the job.

Orson Cart

The group that wasn't fooled did not know the plot of the play or the book, nor did they spot any production flaw.

They were children.

Outstanding

The feature of *The Old Farmer's Almanac* that made it more popular had nothing to do with its printed contents.

It had no value other than as an almanac.

Its advantage was practical.

Paper Tiger

The sheets of paper were important.
He wrote the numbers in ink.

He intended to keep the papers for his later personal use.

He did this each year at a certain time of year.

Plane and Simple

The tree was normal and the boy was normal.

Trees grow differently from boys.

Pork Puzzler

The bacon served a purpose on the journey but was never used as food.

He packed it at the top of his suitcase.

Bacon is offensive to certain people.

∿ Publicity Puzzler

The two men both share a problem. It's an unusual
    problem.

It's not identical for each man.

By shopping together they gain a financial benefit.

They shop for one type of item only. It's not food, furniture,
    or electrical goods.

∿ Quo Vadis?

The archaeologist didn't use any written
    or pictorial evidence.

He deduced that Romans drove their chariots on
    the left-hand side of the road from physical evidence.
    But not from the remains of chariots.

He excavated a Roman quarry.

∿ Rich Man, Poor Man

It has nothing to do with the costs or prices of tea or milk.

It has nothing to do with the taste or flavor of the tea.

It concerns the cups from which they drank their tea.

∿ Rock of Ages

He was oblivious to all around him.

He was struck with a strong blow.

His wife tried to help him.

Running on Empty

Something bad was averted.

Nobody was driving the car when it ran out of gas.

Rush Job

He exploited a different need of the miners.

He turned the tents to some other use—
not accommodation.

The tents were made of heavy denim material.

School's Out

She was instructed to go to school for her education.

She was already very old (and well educated).

She was issued the court order automatically.

The Sealed Room

Nothing else and nobody else was involved
except the man and the sealed room.

He died slowly but not from lack of food, water,
or oxygen. If he had not been in the sealed room,
he would have lived.

Shell Shock

The game is rigged.

The dealer is fast, but it isn't speed alone that deceives
the player.

∾ Sick Leave

Walter was human and physically normal.

The hospital was a normal hospital.

He wasn't able to walk into the hospital or out of it.

∾ Sign Here

He had intended to use the two signs in two places to give
the same message, but he found that that didn't work.

He was advertising his roadside café.

∾ Silly Cone

The office manager found a way for people to waste less time.

The cones were given away free.

A cone will not rest on its end.

∾ The Single Word

Other people also heard what she had to say.

There is no sexual connotation to this story. The narrator
could be male or female.

The word I said summarized a decision that would
significantly affect the woman.

None of my companions was allowed to speak
in the woman's presence.

∾ Small Is Not Beautiful

It doesn't have to do with pollution, crime, economy,
car production, or politics.

The reason concerned safety.

Small cars were more dangerous in certain types
   of accidents that occur often in Sweden.

∾ Smile, Please!

The toothpaste company adopted his idea
   and their sales increased.

It had nothing to do with the taste, price,
   or distribution of the toothpaste.

The idea encouraged people to use more toothpaste.

∾ Spies Are Us

They went to the restaurant as paying customers.

No codes were used, and they never spoke or sat
   near each other.

They dressed in similar clothes.

∾ Stamp Dearth Death

If he had bought the right postage, he would have lived.

He sent a package.

∾ A Strange Collection

The contents are inedible, but they are not bones
   or animal parts.

They had done something relevant together earlier in the day.

They are eating game.

∾ The Stuffed Cloud

The meteorologist died.

He wasn't aware of the stuffed cloud. It hadn't affected any of his forecasts or reports.

He was traveling.

∾ Superior Knowledge

Nobody said anything, but there was visible evidence of the man's presence.

It had nothing to do with shaving.

∾ Surprise Visit

The factory manager and his staff cleared away all the rubbish and left the factory looking spotlessly clean.

The chairman arrived in an unexpected fashion.

He saw a terrible mess.

∾ Throwing His Weight About

The man was normal, fit, and healthy.

He died by accident.

He was trying to demonstrate something.

∾ Tittle Tattle

Tittles are seen in print.

There are two in this sentence.

∾ Top at Last

William didn't cheat.

He didn't revise or work any harder than usual.

He wasn't particularly happy to be top of the list.

∾ The Tracks of My Tires

The police didn't ask any questions but merely used their powers of observation.

When the police arrived, none of the three suspects was carrying a weapon or wearing blood-stained clothing.

The police correctly deduced that the woman was the murderer.

∾ Turned Off

The man didn't interfere with the physical operation of the radio stations.

There was no threat or misinformation.

All radio stations voluntarily chose to stop transmitting for a short period.

∾ 2020 Vision

The farmer was being truthful.

Exactly 22 pigs were stolen.

∽ Two Pigs

They were sold on the same day at the same market.

Each was sold for a fair price.

The two pigs looked the same, but when they were sold one was worth much more than the other.

One was sold for food—the other was not.

∽ Unfinished Business

The work isn't necessarily big.

Many people undertake this work.

None of them can ever truly complete it.

∽ Up in Smoke

The cigars were valuable. He didn't steal or sell them.

He was perfectly entitled to smoke them.

He successfully claimed the $10,000 and, as a result, was found guilty of a crime.

∽ The Upset Bird-Watcher

The bird was just as beautiful and rare as he had imagined. He wasn't disappointed with its appearance.

What happened to the bird placed him at risk.

He saw the bird through a small window.

∿ The Upset Woman

He was an unwelcome intruder.

He had visited before, so she left some food for him.

She wanted him to die.

∿ Vase and Means

They discovered the ingredient by accident.

The ingredient strengthened the pottery.

The accident was a tragedy.

∿ What's the Point?

A round pencil would not do.

She hates losing pencils.

∿ Who Did It?

The teacher didn't threaten or bribe any child.

No child admitted the misdemeanor or tattled
on anyone else.

The teacher gave the class an exercise to do.

∿ Wonderful Weather

The accident happened at night.

No other craft was involved.

The accident happened in winter.

∾ **Written Down**

She is writing in an unusual place.

She has difficulty writing the letters P, R, T, and Z,
    but no difficulty with O, Q, S, U, X, and Y.

She is writing on thick books.

∾ **Wrong Way**

The man had a rational reason for choosing a bus going
    in the opposite direction to the one he wanted.

His reason was not to do with saving money, saving time,
    avoiding danger, seeing anything, or meeting anyone.

His reason has to do with comfort.

SUPER PUZZLES

VIEW FROM ALL ANGLES

THE DEADLY SCULPTURE

A penniless sculptor made a beautiful metal statue, which he sold. Because of this he died soon afterward. Why?

Clues: 142/Answer: 245.

PEAK PERFORMANCE

The body of a climber is found many years after his death a thousand feet below the summit of one of the world's highest mountains. In his pocket is a diary claiming that he had reached the summit and was on his way down. How was it discovered that he was not telling the truth?

Clues: 251/Answer: 250.

THE FATAL FISH

A man was preparing a fish to eat for a meal when he made a mistake. He then knew that he would shortly die. How?

Clues: 145/Answer: 247.

ADAM HAD NONE

Adam had none. Eve had two. Everyone nowadays has three. What are they?

Clues: 139/Answer: 243.

SHOT DEAD

A woman who was in a house saw a stranger walking down the road. She took a gun and shot him dead. The next day she did the same thing to another stranger. Other people saw her do it and knew that she had killed the two men, yet she was never arrested or charged. Why not?

Clues: 155/Answer: 253.

WOULD YOU BELIEVE IT?

Three people were holding identical blocks of wood. They released the blocks at the same time. The blocks of wood were not attached to anything. The first person's block fell downward. The second person's block rose up. The third person's block stayed where it was, unsupported. What was going on?

Clues: 160/Answer: 256.

JAILBREAK

A man planned his escape from prison very carefully. He could have carried it out in the dead of night, but he preferred to do it in the middle of the morning. Why?

Clues: 147/Answer: 248.

SITTING DUCKS

Why does a woman with no interest in hunting buy a gun for shooting ducks? *Clues: 155/Answer: 253.*

BALD FACTS

Mary, Queen of Scots was almost totally bald, and wore a wig to conceal this fact from her subjects. How was her secret revealed?

Clues: 140/Answer: 244.

LETHAL ACTION

Brazilian authorities took actions to protect their fruit crops, and ten people from another continent died. How?

Clues:148/Answer: 248.

RECOGNITION

John lived in England all his life, until his parents died. He then went to Australia to visit relatives. His Aunt Mary had left England before he was born and had never returned. He had never met his Aunt Mary, had never spoken to her, and had never seen a picture of her. Yet he recognized her immediately in a crowded airport. How?

Clues: 153/Answer: 252.

DESTRUCTION

Commercial premises are destroyed by a customer. Afterward, he disappears, but even if he had been caught he could not have been charged. Why?

Clues: 143/Answer: 245.

WONDERFUL WALK

A man and his dog went for a walk in the woods. When he returned home he invented something now worth millions of dollars. What was it?

Clues: 159/Answer: 255.

PESKY ESCALATOR

A foreign visitor to London wanted to ride up the escalator at the subway station, but did not do so. Why?

Clues: 151/Answer: 251.

POLES APART

How did early explorers economize with provisions for a polar expedition?

Clues: 151/Answer: 251.

ARRESTED DEVELOPMENT

A bank robber grabbed several thousand dollars from a bank counter and, although he was armed, he was captured within a few seconds before he could leave the bank. How?

Clues: 139/Answer: 243.

HOLED OUT

A golfer dreamed all his life of getting a hole in one. However, when he eventually did get a hole in one, he was very unhappy and, in fact, quit golf altogether. Why?

Clues: 147/Answer: 248.

TRUNK-ATED

The police stop a car and they suspect that the trunk contains evidence linking the driver with a serious crime. However, they do not have a search warrant, and if they open the trunk forcibly without probable cause, any evidence uncovered will not be admissible in court. How do they proceed?

Clues: 157/Answer: 254.

SPORTS MAD

Why was a keen sports fan rushing around his house looking for a roll of sticky tape? *Clues: 156/Answer: 253.*

APPENDECTOMY I & II

(There are two different solutions to this puzzle. Try both of them before looking at the answer to either.) Why did a surgeon remove a perfectly healthy appendix?

Clues: 139/Answer: 243.

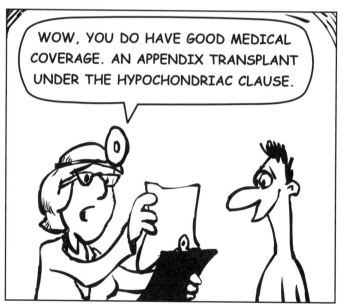

RIOTOUS ASSEMBLY

After riots in a large institution, one section did not reopen for a long time after the other sections. Why?

Clues: 153/Answer: 252.

KNEED TO KNOW

A woman places her hand on her husband's knee for an hour and then takes it off for ten minutes; then she places her hand on her husband's knee for another hour. Why?

Clues: 148/Answer: 248.

BAD TRIP

An anti-drug agency distributed material to children in school. However, this had the opposite effect to what was intended. Why?

Clues: 140/Answer: 244.

WALLY TEST III

WALLY Test time rolls around once again. You know the drill—they may seem easy, but be on your guard. Write down your answers on a piece of paper, and then see how many you got right. The time limit is three minutes.

1. When you see geese flying in a V formation, why is it that one leg of the V is always longer than the other?

2. Why are there so many Smiths in the telephone directory?

3. What is E.T. short for?

4. Where do you find a no-legged dog?

5. Approximately how many house bricks does it take to complete a brick house in England?

6. How do you stop a bull from charging?

7. What cheese is made backward?

8. Take away my first letter; I remain the same.
Now, take away my fourth letter; I remain the same.
Now, take away my last letter; I remain the same.
What am I?

9. If a white man threw a black stone into the Red Sea, what would it become?

10. How do you make a bandstand?

Answers on page 257.

THINK OUT OF THE BOX

SHOE SHOP SHUFFLE

In a small town there are four shoe shops of about the same size, each carrying more or less the same line in shoes. Yet, one shop loses three times as many shoes to theft as each of the other shops. Why?

Clues: 154/Answer: 252.

DRIVING AWAY

A man steals a very expensive car owned by a very rich woman. Although he was a very good driver, within a few minutes, he was involved in a serious accident. Why?

Clues: 143/Answer: 246.

LIT TOO WELL?

Local government authorities in Sussex, England, installed many more lights than were needed. This resulted in considerable damage, but the authorities were pleased with the results. Why?

Clues: 148/Answer: 249.

CAESAR'S BLUNDER

Julius Caesar unexpectedly lost many of his ships when he invaded Britain. Why?

Clues: 141/Answer: 244.

SLOW DEATH

The ancient Greek playwright Aeschylus was killed by a tortoise. How?

Clues: 155/Answer: 253.

QUICK ON THE DRAW

Every Saturday night, the national lottery is drawn with a multimillion-dollar first prize. A man sat down in front of his TV on Saturday night and saw that the numbers drawn exactly matched the numbers on his ticket for that day's lottery. He was thrilled, but did not win a penny. Why not?

Clues: 153/Answer: 251.

SCALED DOWN

A butcher tried to deceive a customer by pressing down on the scale while weighing a turkey to make it appear heavier than it was. But the customer's subsequent order forced the butcher to admit his deception. How?

Clues: 154/Answer: 252.

THE HAPPY WOMAN

A woman going on a journey used a driver. Then she stopped and used a club to hit a large bird. She was very pleased. Why?

Clues: 146/Answer: 248.

VANDAL SCANDAL

The authorities in Athens were very concerned that tourists sometimes hacked pieces of marble from the columns of the ancient Parthenon buildings. The practice was illegal, but some people seemed determined to take away souvenirs. How did the authorities stop this vandalism?

Clues: 158/Answer: 255.

THE DEADLY DRAWING

A woman walked into a room and saw a new picture there. She immediately knew that someone had been killed. How?

Clues: 142/Answer: 245.

DOWN PERISCOPE

A normal submarine was on the surface of the sea with its hatches open. It sailed due east for two miles. Then it stopped and went down 30 feet. It then sailed another half mile before going down a further 30 feet. All this time it kept its hatches fully open. The crew survived and were not alarmed in any way. What was going on?

Clues: 143/Answer: 246.

THE LETTER LEFT OUT

For mathematical reasons, in codes and ciphers it is desirable to have 25 (which is a perfect square) letters rather than the usual 26. Which letter of the English alphabet is left out and why?

Clues: 148/Answer: 249.

ARRESTED DEVELOPMENT—AGAIN

Two masked men robbed a bank, but they were very quickly picked up by the police. Why?

Clues: 140/Answer: 243.

TITANIC PROPORTIONS

How did the sinking of the *Titanic* lead directly to the sinking of another ship?
Clues: 157/Answer: 254.

THE MOVER

What can go from there to here by disappearing and then go from here to there by appearing?

Clues: 149/Answer: 250.

NEW WORLD RECORD

A 102-year-old woman was infirm and inactive, yet, one day she was congratulated on setting a new world record. What was it?

Clues: 150/Answer: 250.

DEATH OF A PLAYER

A sportsman was rushed to a hospital from where he was playing and died, shortly afterward. Why?

Clues: 143/Answer: 245.

AVOID ASSUMPTIONS

DEATH BY ROMANCE

A newly married couple had a fireside supper together. They were so cozy and comfortable that they dozed off on the floor. Next morning they were both found dead where they lay. What had happened?

Clues: 142/Answer: 245.

PENALTY

After a World Cup soccer match, two players swapped jerseys. The police immediately arrested them. Why?

Clues: 151/Answer: 250.

GOLF CHALLENGE I, II, & III

(There are three different solutions to this puzzle. Try all three of them before looking at any of the answers.)

A man and a woman, who were both poor golfers, challenged each other to a match. The man scored 96 while the woman scored 98. However, the woman was declared the winner. Why?

Clues: 146/Answer: 247.

POOR INVESTMENT

A man bought a house for $1 million as an investment. The house was well kept and carefully maintained by a good caretaker. Although the house remained in perfect structural order, within a few years it was worthless. Why?

Clues: 152/Answer: 251.

GIVE US A HAND . . .

A man searching for precious stones didn't find any, but found a severed human hand instead. What had happened?

Clues: 146/Answer: 247.

EVIL INTENT

A rich man meets a lady during intermission at the theater and invites her back to his house for a drink. She has a drink and then leaves. About an hour later he suddenly realizes that she intends to return and burgle his house. How does he know?

Clues: 144/Answer: 246.

TWO HEADS ARE BETTER THAN ONE!

Several Americans reported they saw a creature that had two heads, two arms, and four legs. They were surprised, frightened, and alarmed, and when they told their friends, nobody believed them. But they were reliable witnesses. What had they seen?

Clues: 157/Answer: 254.

STONE ME!

A boy flung a stone at a man and many people's lives were saved. How come?

Clues: 156/Answer: 253.

JUDGE FOR YOURSELF

The defendant in a major lawsuit asked his lawyer if he should send the judge a box of fine cigars in the hope of influencing him. The lawyer said that was a very bad idea and it would prejudice the judge against him. The defendant listened carefully, sent the cigars, and won the case. What happened?

Clues: 147/Answer: 248.

LOVE LETTERS

Why did a woman send out 1,000 anonymous Valentine's cards to different men?

Clues: 148/Answer: 249.

STRANGE BEHAVIOR

A man was driving down the road into town with his family on a clear day. He saw a tree and immediately stopped the car and then reversed at high speed. Why?

Clues: 156/Answer: 253.

TREE TROUBLE

The authorities were concerned that a famous old tree was being damaged because so many tourists came up to it and touched it. So a wall was built around the tree to protect it. But this had the opposite effect of that intended. Why?

Clues: 157/Answer: 254.

THE BURIAL CHAMBER

Why did a man build a beautiful burial chamber, complete with sculptures and paintings, and then deliberately wreck it?

Clues: 141/Answer: 244.

MISCARRIAGE OF JUSTICE

An Italian judge released a guilty man and convicted an innocent man. As a result the confectionery industry has greatly benefited. Why is that?

Clues: 149/Answer: 249.

OFFENSES DOWN

The police in Sussex, England, found a new way to complete their form-filling and paperwork that significantly reduced crime. What was it?

Clues: 150/Answer: 250.

POLICE CHASE

A high-speed police car chases a much slower vehicle in which criminals are escaping. But the police fail to catch them. Why?

Clues: 152/Answer: 251.

CAFÉ SOCIETY

A small café is pestered by teenagers who come in, buy a single cup of coffee, and then stay for hours, cutting down on available space for other patrons. How does the owner get rid of them, quite legally?

Clues: 141/Answer: 244.

HI, JEAN!

A shop owner introduced expensive new procedures to make his premises more hygienic, but the results were the very opposite. Why is that?

Clues: 147/Answer: 248.

THE EMPTY MACHINE

A gumball machine dispensed gum when quarters were inserted. When the machine was opened, there was no money inside. A considerable number of gumballs had been consumed, and the machine did not appear to have been interfered with in any way. What had happened?

Clues: 144/Answer: 246.

TAKE A FENCE

A man painted his garden fence green and then went on holiday. When he came back two weeks later, he was amazed to see that the fence was blue. Nobody had touched the fence. What had happened?

Clues: 156/Answer: 254.

WALLY TEST IV

Ready? Aim . . . WALLY Test! Your mind should be pretty on-target by now. Write down your answers on a piece of paper, and then see how many you got right. The time limit is three minutes.

1.   What should you give an injured lemon?

2.   If an atheist died in church, what would they put on his coffin?

3.   Who was it that went into the lion's den unarmed and came out alive?

4.   A man rode down the street on a horse, yet walked. How come?

5.   How can you eat an egg without breaking the shell?

6.   Why was King Henry VIII buried in Westminster Abbey?

7.   In China they hang many criminals, but they will not hang a man with a wooden leg. Why?

8.   Why do storks stand on one leg?

9.   A circular field is covered in thick snow. A black cow with white spots is in the middle. Two white cows with black spots are on the edge of the field. What time is it?

10. What was the problem with the wooden car with wooden wheels and a wooden engine?

Answers on page 258.

CHANGE PERSPECTIVES

SEX DISCRIMINATION

When lawyers went to prison to visit their clients, they found that female lawyers were searched on entry but male lawyers were not. Why?

Clues: 154/Answer: 252.

WEIGHT LOSS

How did a Japanese diet clinic achieve great weight-loss results for its patients even though they did not change their diet or undertake more activity than normal?

Clues: 159/Answer: 255.

PSYCHIC

You enter a parking lot and see a woman walking toward you. You then see a row of cars and know immediately which one is hers. How?

Clues: 152/Answer: 251.

THE HAPPY ROBBER

A robber holds up a bank, but leaves with no money whatsoever. However, he is more pleased than if he had left with lots of money. Why is that?

Clues: 146/Answer: 247.

SIEGE MENTALITY

A city is under siege. The attackers have run out of ammunition and have suffered heavy casualties. Yet they take the city within a few days without further losses. How?

Clues: 155/Answer: 253.

CARRIER BAGS

During World War II, the British Royal Navy had very few aircraft carriers. What ingenious plan was devised to remedy this deficiency?

Clues: 141/Answer: 244.

THE CATHEDRAL UNTOUCHED

When London was bombed during World War II, St. Paul's Cathedral, in the center of the city, was never hit. Why not?

Clues: 142/Answer: 245.

BAGS AWAY

An airplane nearly crashed because one of the passengers had not fastened his suitcase securely enough. What happened?

Clues: 140/Answer: 244.

THE SAD SAMARITAN

Jim saw a stranded motorist on a country road. The motorist had run out of fuel, so Jim took him to the nearest garage and then drove him back to his car. Jim felt good that he had been such a good Samaritan, but discovered something later that made him very sad. What was it?

Clues: 154/Answer: 252.

THE TALLEST TREE

Men found what they suspected was the tallest tree in Australia. It was growing in the outback in rough terrain and with other trees around. They did not have any advanced instruments with them. How did they accurately measure the height of the tree?

Clues: 157/Answer: 254.

THE UNWELCOME GUEST

A couple had a neighbor who continually arrived at mealtimes in the hope of getting a free meal. How did they use their very friendly dog to persuade the neighbor not to come for free meals again?   *Clues: 158/Answer: 254.*

POOR SHOW

Every time he performed in public, it was a complete flop. Yet, he became famous for it, and won medals and prizes. People came from all over and paid to see him perform. Who was he?

Clues: 152/Answer: 251.

MESSAGE RECEIVED

How did Alexander the Great send secret messages with his envoy?

Clues: 149/Answer: 249.

THE MIGHTY STONE

There was a huge boulder in the middle of a village green. It was too big to be moved, too hard to split, and dynamiting it was too dangerous. How did a simple peasant suggest getting rid of it?

Clues: 149/Answer: 249.

THE WORLD'S MOST EXPENSIVE CAR

The most expensive car ever made is for sale. Although many people want to own it and can afford to buy it, nobody will do so. Why? *Clues: 159/Answer: 256.*

THE FATAL FALL

A woman dropped a piece of wood. She picked it up again and carried on as if nothing had happened. The wood was not damaged and she was not injured, but the incident cost her her life. Why?

Clues: 145/Answer: 246.

ELECTION SELECTION

There is an election in a deprived city area. All the political parties put up candidates, actively canvass, and spend money on their campaigns. Yet, the election is won by a candidate who did not canvass or advertise and is unknown to all of the electors. How?

Clues: 144/Answer: 246.

WELL TRAINED

A man, a woman, and a child are watching a train come into a station. "Here it comes," says the man. "Here she comes," says the woman. "Here he comes," says the child. Who is correct?

Clues: 159/Answer: 255.

RAZOR ATTACK

A man had his throat attacked by a woman with a razor, yet he suffered no serious injuries. How come?

Clues: 153/Answer: 252.

THE OLD CROONER

How did Bing Crosby reduce the crime rate in various U.S. cities?

Clues: 150/Answer: 250.

GENEROSITY?

A man took considerable trouble to acquire some money, but then quickly gave most of it away. Why?

Clues: 145/Answer: 247.

THE PARSON'S PUP

Why did the vicar want only a black dog?

Clues: 150/Answer: 250.

WATCH THAT MAN!

A runner was awarded a prize for winning a marathon. But the judges disqualified him when they saw a picture of his wristwatch. Why?

Clues: 158/Answer: 255.

CLUES TO SUPER PUZZLES

∾ **Adam Had None**

It has nothing to do with family, relations, bones,
or physical appearance.

It has to do with names.

∾ **Appendectomy I & II**

No financial gain is involved in either solution.

The doctors who removed the healthy appendixes acted out
of good motives.

Both solutions involve situations in the first part
of the 20th century.

∾ **Arrested Development**

The robber wanted to get out of the bank as quickly
as he could.

There was nothing particularly noticeable or remarkable
about the bank robber that would make him easy
to identify.

He was not very bright.

∿ Arrested Development—Again

The robbers wore masks so as not to be recognized.

They made a clean getaway.

Bank employees noticed something about the two men.

The men were brothers.

∿ Bad Trip

The anti-drug agency wanted actively to promote a message that drugs were bad, but inadvertently they ended up promoting the opposite message.

The agency distributed pencils to children and the children used them.

∿ Bags Away

The passenger's suitcase was stored in the hold of the plane.

He was not a terrorist or criminal.

The passenger's suitcase did not contain chemicals, explosives, or drugs.

∿ Bald Facts

Mary, Queen of Scots took great care never to be seen without her wig.

Her wig was very good and looked completely natural.

Although Mary, Queen of Scots never wanted to be seen without her wig, she was not upset or embarrassed when it eventually happened, even though many people saw it.

∾ The Burial Chamber

The burial chamber wasn't built for use by the builder.

He wrecked it before anyone was buried there.

He did not wreck it out of spite or anger.
> He deliberately destroyed it to deceive.

He wrecked the chamber to save the chamber.

∾ Caesar's Blunder

The sea was calm and there were no storms when Caesar
> sailed across the channel and arrived in Britain.

He arrived safely and disembarked his troops
> and equipment.

Caesar had never visited Britain before.

He had learned to sail in the Mediterranean.

∾ Café Society

The café owner did not change the menu or prices or music
> in the café.

He changed the appearance of the café in a way that
> embarrassed the teenagers.

∾ Carrier Bags

The suggestion was a way of creating new aircraft carriers
> much more cheaply than by the conventional methods.

It would possibly have been practical in the North Atlantic.

They were disposable carriers.

∾ The Cathedral Untouched

The area all around St. Paul's was heavily bombed,
    but it appeared that no bombs could fall on St. Paul's.

The German bombers deliberately avoided bombing it.

They were not acting out of any religious or moral principles.

∾ The Deadly Drawing

She was correct in her deduction that someone
    had been killed.

She did not know the person who had been killed,
    who had killed them, nor how they had died.

She had never been in that room before,
    and she had not seen the picture before.

∾ The Deadly Sculpture

He lived a lonely life in a remote building.

He made the statue out of copper. It was taken far away,

and he never saw it again.

He died as the result of an accident. No other person,
    animal, or sculpture was involved.

∾ Death by Romance

They did not die of food or gas poisoning, nor from the
    effects of any kind of exertion.

They were not murdered. They died by accident.

They were in an unusual house.

∿ **Death of a Player**

The man was not involved in any collisions or tackles
and did not suffer any injuries, yet it was because
of his sport that he accidentally died.

He was a golfer, but he was not hit by a club, a ball,
or indeed by anything.

If only he had put his tee in his pocket!

∿ **Destruction**

The customer was a man who accidentally destroyed
the premises without knowing that he was doing so.

He was there the whole time that the premises
were being destroyed.

He was very overweight.

∿ **Down Periscope**

The submarine was in water at all times and was not on
dry ground or in dry dock.

No water entered the submarine.

This could happen only in certain places, and not in
the open sea.

∿ **Driving Away**

Driving conditions were excellent, but the thief
found the woman's car very difficult to drive.

She had had the car modified.

The rich woman suffered from some of the same frailties
as other old people.

There was nothing unusual about the car's engine, gears,
wheels, steering, or bodywork.

❧ Election Selection

The successful candidate had no particular experience,
qualifications, or characteristics that qualified him for
the job or increased his appeal to voters.

He did not canvass, advertise, or spend money in any way

to influence the voters, and he remained unknown
to the voters.

The other candidates were competent and trustworthy
and did nothing to disqualify themselves.

He changed something about himself.

❧ The Empty Machine

Kids had cheated the gum company.

They had not put quarters into the machine,
but they had obtained gumballs.

The machine was rusty, but it still worked fine.

❧ Evil Intent

It was nothing she said or did with the man.
He did not remember anything to cause his realization
that she planned to burglerize him.

He noticed something.

While he was preparing the drinks, she did something.

He had his hands full.

∾ The Fatal Fall

The woman wasn't a criminal, and no crime was involved.

She was quite upset to have dropped the piece of wood.

The wood was a cylinder about one foot long.

The piece of wood was not particularly valuable
and could easily be replaced.

Many people saw her drop the piece of wood.

∾ The Fatal Fish

The man died in an accident. He was not poisoned or stabbed.

No other person was involved. No crime was involved.

The man did not eat the fish. The type of fish is irrelevant.
It was dead.

He was not indoors.

∾ Generosity?

He had not intended to give any money away, and did not
do so out of altruistic motives.

He was under pressure.

∾ Give Us a Hand …

The man whose hand it was had also been looking
for precious stones.

He had been forced to cut off his own hand.

To find these precious stones, men needed strong limbs,
good eyes, good lungs, and great fitness.

∾ Golf Challenge I, II, & III

I. The woman's gender was no handicap.

II. The woman was more than a match for the man.

III. It was a very wet day, and the golf course was
flooded.

∾ The Happy Robber

He was poor. He stole something from the bank,
but it was not money.

He made no financial gain from the theft. He stole for love.

He stole a rare liquid.

∾ The Happy Woman

Although she used a driver, she walked about four miles
in the course of her tour.

She wore special shoes.

She saw many flags.

∿ Hi, Jean!

The shop owner sold food, and he wanted to present it
    in the best possible light.

He took action to deter and kill pests.

∿ Holed Out

It was not a good shot that got him the hole in one.

He should have been more careful.

The golfer's ball rebounded into the hole.

Another person was involved.

∿ Jailbreak

There was an advantage to him in escaping in the morning.
        It had nothing to do with light, deliveries,
        or prison-officer routines.

He did not want to be spotted once he was outside the prison.

He knew that his escape would be detected after about
    half an hour.

∿ Judge for Yourself

The defendant's actions probably influenced the judge
    in his favor.

The judge was scrupulously honest and would resent any
    intent to bribe or influence him.

∿ Kneed to Know

The man and his wife were in a room full of people.

She put her hand on his knee not as a sign of affection
or encouragement but as an act of communication.

He gained an understanding through her actions.

∿ Lethal Action

The dead people were Africans. They didn't eat the fruit.

The Brazilian authorities' actions involved pesticides.

The Africans acted illegally. Their deaths were accidents.

∿ The Letter Left Out

The letter that is left out is chosen not because
it is rarely used but because it is easily substituted
without any risk of misunderstanding.

∿ Lit Too Well?

The authorities deliberately set up lights in fields
and on roads, even though people living there
had not requested them and did not need them.

There was damage to fields, crops, roads,
and farm animals, as a result.

Overall, though, human lives were saved.

∿ Love Letters

She didn't know the men and didn't like any of them.

She had malicious intentions.

There was potential financial gain for her.

∿ **Message Received**

Envoys were thoroughly searched when they arrived
at a foreign location to check for hidden messages.

The envoys did not memorize the messages or ever know
or see the contents of the messages.

The messages were hidden on the person of the envoy but
they could not be seen, even when the envoy was
naked.

∿ **The Mighty Stone**

The peasant did not suggest building over it.

He suggested a way of moving the stone, but not by pushing it
or pulling it.

He used its own weight to help move it.

∿ **Miscarriage of Justice**

The Italian judge tried a rebel, but released a robber.

The Italian was not in Italy when he made the judgment.

The judge, the rebel, and the robber never ate any chocolate.

∿ **The Mover**

It is something you see every day.

In fact, you have seen one in the last few seconds.

∾ New World Record

She did not do anything physical.

She became the only known person to achieve a certain feat.

It was not her age alone that did this,
    though one would have to be old to do it.

∾ Offenses Down

The police officers filled in their reports and forms
        in a different fashion, which reduced crime,
        but they did not fill them in any better, quicker, more
        accurately, or with more information than before.

They filled in the reports by hand, not by computer.

The key difference was their location when they
        did the paperwork.

∾ The Old Crooner

Bing Crosby himself did not take part in the action
        to reduce crime.

His songs were used to reduce crime.

His songs are old-fashioned and melodic, which means
        that some people like them and some do not.

∾ The Parson's Pup

The fact that he is religious is not relevant.

The vicar is particular about his appearance.

∿ Peak Performance

He had been dead for many years, so it was not possible
to tell from his physical condition or clothing whether
he had reached the summit.

The manner of his death is not relevant.

No camera was involved.

What would he have done had he reached the summit?

∿ Penalty

It was a regular soccer match played in the World Cup
in front of thousands of people.

The players were not criminals or terrorists—
just soccer players.

The match was played in an Arab country.

∿ Pesky Escalator

There was no one else around.

The foreign visitor saw a sign.

He was very obedient.

∿ Poles Apart

The explorers knew that there would be no sources of food,
other than what they carried with them.

They did something that would not normally be
considered a good idea.

∾ Police Chase

The fast police car was right behind the criminals' vehicle,
and there was no other traffic or vehicle involved.
The roads were clear and the weather was fine.

The getaway vehicle was a bus.

The bus driver was number seven.

∾ Poor Investment

There were no other buildings nearby, and no buildings
or roads were added or removed in the vicinity.

There were no earthquakes, floods, fires, or eruptions,
and no damage by trees or vegetation.

The house had a beautiful view.

∾ Poor Show

His performances were always a flop,
but he was very successful.

He was not in comedy, music, cinema, or theater.

His most famous performance was in Mexico.

He was a sportsman.

∾ Psychic

You see the cars after you see the woman, and you did not
see her leaving the car.

There is something different in the appearance of her car.

She is carrying something.

∽ Quick on the Draw

He had a perfectly valid ticket for that day's lottery;
he was not a prizewinner.

He saw the exact numbers on his ticket
come up on the TV show.

He had a cruel wife.

∽ Razor Attack

She meant to hurt him, and he did not defend himself.

The razor made full contact with his unprotected throat.

She could not have shaved him, either.

∽ Recognition

His Aunt Mary was not carrying a sign or wearing
anything distinctive. She did not have any disabilities
or characteristics that would make her stand out.

He had not arranged to meet her in a specific place
or asked her to wear or carry anything in particular.

He recognized her from her facial appearance.

∽ Riotous Assembly

The section did not have the equipment it needed to reopen.

The rioters had used everything they could lay their hands on.

The police had intervened but were driven back
when the rioters threw rocks at them.

∿ The Sad Samaritan

Jim was not robbed or deceived by the motorist in any way.

Jim tried his best to help, but failed.

The motorist was stranded.

∿ Scaled Down

The butcher had only one turkey left.

He weighed it for the customer.

He pressed down on the scale with his thumb
to give it an exaggerated weight.

∿ Sex Discrimination

The prison guards were not acting in a discriminatory,
sexist, or unfair fashion, but simply
following procedures.

Women were more likely to fall afoul
of the security equipment.

∿ Shoe Shop Shuffle

The four shops have similar staffing, lighting,
and security arrangements.

The shop that suffers the heaviest thefts is not in a worse
part of town or in an environment that is more
popular with criminals.

The shop that suffers the heaviest thefts does something
different with its shoes.

∾ **Shot Dead**

> The woman and the strangers were neither criminals
> nor police.

> The strangers did not see the woman and did not know
> that she was in the house.

> The strangers were armed and were a threat to the woman.

∾ **Siege Mentality**

> This took place in the Middle Ages.

> The defenders had plenty of food, water, and ammunition.

> The attackers had catapulted rocks over the walls,
> but had now run out of ammunition.

∾ **Sitting Ducks**

> The woman loves animals and hates hunting.
> > She does not intend to use the gun for hunting
> > or for self-defense.

> There is no criminal intent in mind.

> The ducks are already dead when she shoots them.

∾ **Slow Death**

> Aeschylus did not trip over the tortoise or slip on it.

> He did not eat it or attempt to eat it. He was not poisoned
> or bitten by the tortoise.

> No other human was involved in his death.

∾ Sports Mad

The sports fan was not exercising. He was not injured.
He wanted the tape because of his sports obsession.

No sports equipment is involved.

He was a football fan. He followed his team fanatically
but rarely got the chance to go to the games.

∾ Stone Me!

The man was much bigger than the boy.

The stone hit the man on the head.

Many people watched.

∾ Strange Behavior

There were many trees along the side of the road. The man
had never seen or noticed this tree before.

There was something different about this tree.

His primary concern was safety.

The tree itself was not a threat to him.

∾ Take a Fence

No other person or animal was involved.

The change in color was not caused by the sun or wind.

The change in color was caused by the rain,
but every other house and fence in the area
remained unchanged in color.

∾ The Tallest Tree

The men did not use angles or shadows.

They did not climb the tree.

They measured it accurately using rope and measuring lines.

∾ Titanic Proportions

The ship that sank was not involved in the sinking
of the Titanic or the rescue operation.

Laws were passed to ensure that ships improved their safety.

One ship sank, but all the passengers were saved.

∾ Tree Trouble

The wall successfully kept prying people
away from the tree—just as intended.

The tree died.

∾ Trunk-ated

The policeman is able to prove that there is something
suspicious in the trunk, without opening it.

He suspects that there is a body in the trunk.

How do you attempt to contact a dead man?

∾ Two Heads Are Better Than One!

They were not drunk or under any strange influence.

This happened in North America.

They had seen a creature they had never seen before.

∿ The Unwelcome Guest

The neighbor liked the dog,
    and the dog did not annoy the neighbor.

The couple gave the neighbor a fine meal.

He was horrified at what happened next.

∿ Vandal Scandal

The authorities did not add extra security or protection
    for the ancient buildings.

They fooled the people who were determined
    to take souvenirs.

Tourists went away happy.

∿ Watch That Man!

The wristwatch was perfectly legal and did not give
    the runner an unfair advantage.

The man had cheated.

The clue to his cheating was that his wristwatch
    had changed hands.

∾ Weight Loss

The diet and the daily regimen were not changed.
But something else about the clinic was changed,
and this produced the weight loss in patients.

The change made the patients work a little harder
in normal activities.

The fact that the clinic is in Japan is not particularly
relevant. Similar results could have been obtained
in many countries—but not in Belgium or Holland.

∾ Well Trained

Do not take this puzzle too seriously—it involves a bad pun.

The child was correct. But why?

∾ Wonderful Walk

Something annoying happened during the walk in the woods.

It gave the man an idea.

He invented a popular fastener.

∾ The World's Most Expensive Car

The car was used once and is in good condition, but it has
not been driven for many years.

Most people have seen it on TV, but they can't name
the man who drove it.

It is not associated with any celebrity or with any
remarkable historical event or tragedy,
though when it was driven it was a special event at the
time.

It was developed at great expense for practical use
and not for show or exhibition.

∿ **Would You Believe It?**

The blocks of wood were identical
and so were the people (for the purposes of this puzzle),
but their circumstances were not identical.

Normal forces were at work in all three cases—
nothing unusual was going on.

PERPLEXING

PUZZLES

AQUAMARINE

THE LATE REPORT

A man and his wife went on vacation. Two months later, the man called the police to report the location of a body near the place where he had been on holiday. The police thanked the man and then asked why it had taken him two months to report the body. What was the reason?

Clues: 203/Answer: 265.

THE STRANGER IN THE BAR

Two men went out for a drink together in a bar. One of them looked up, saw a tall, dark stranger looking like death and drinking soda water, and pointed him out to his companion. Startled and uneasy, the two men left and went to another bar some miles away. After a few minutes, they looked up and saw the same sad, pale stranger drinking soda water. Deciding to leave, they went to a third bar, which was empty except for a young couple. However, within a few minutes, the cadaverous man appeared and, in a slow, sad voice, ordered a soda water. Almost out of his mind, one of the men went over to him and said, "Who are you and what do you want?" What did the man answer?

Clues: 208/Answer: 269.

GERTRUDE

When Gertrude entered the plane she caused her own death and the deaths of 200 people. Yet she was never blamed or criticized for her actions. What happened?

Clues: 202/Answer: 264.

MAD COW IDEAS

In 1996, the British government was faced with the task of slaughtering many thousands of healthy cattle in order to allay fears over the disease BSE, or mad cow disease. What proposal did the government of Cambodia make to help solve the problem?

Clues: 204/Answer: 266.

THE KING'S FAVOR

When King Charles II of England visited a College at the University of Cambridge, he noticed a fine portrait of his father, King Charles I, hanging in the Main Hall. He asked if he could have it, but the ruling body of the College was very reluctant to part with it. At last the King said that he would grant the College anything in his power if they would give him the portrait and that he would be very displeased and unhelpful if they declined this generous offer. The College elders accepted. What did they ask for in return?

Clues: 203/Answer: 265.

PRICE TAG

Many shops have prices set just under a round figure, e.g., $9.99 instead of $10 or $99.95 instead of $100. It is assumed that this is done because the price seems lower to the consumer. But this is not the reason the practice started. What was the original reason for this pricing method?

Clues: 206/Answer: 268.

COLOR-BLIND

John was color-blind. Because of this affliction, he landed an important job. What was it?

Clues: 198/Answer: 260.

SEASIDE IDEA

A military commander during World War II was on leave, so he took his children to the seaside for a day. Here, he got the idea he needed to carry out his next assignment successfully. What was the idea?

Clues: 207/Answer: 268.

THE HAMMER

Adam was jealous of Brenda's use of a computer. He changed that by means of a hammer. After that, he could use the computer, but Brenda could not. What did he do?

Clues: 202/Answer: 264.

THE STRANGER IN THE HOTEL

A woman was sitting in her hotel room when there was a knock at the door. She opened the door to see a man whom she had never seen before. He said, "Oh, I'm sorry. I have made a mistake. I thought this was my room." He then went off down the corridor to the elevator. The woman went back into her room and phoned reception to ask them to apprehend the man, who she was sure was a thief. What made her so sure?

Clues: 209/Answer: 269.

BUTTONS

There is a reason why men's clothes have buttons on the right while women's have buttons on the left. What is it?

Clues: 197/Answer: 259.

UPSTAIRS, DOWNSTAIRS

In a very exclusive restaurant several dozen diners are eating a top-class meal upstairs. Downstairs, precisely the same meal is being served at the same number of empty places where there is nobody to eat it. What is going on?

Clues: 210/Answer: 271.

SOUPER

A woman was at an expensive and prestigious dinner. The first course was soup. Halfway through the course, she called over a waiter and whispered in his ear. He brought a drinking straw, which she used to finish her soup. The other guests were surprised at her actions, but she had a good explanation. What was it?

Clues: 208/Answer: 269.

EARLY MORNING IN LAS VEGAS

A gambler went to Las Vegas. He won on the roulette table, lost at blackjack, and won at poker. When he went to bed in his hotel room, he carefully double-locked his door. At 3 a.m. he was awakened by the sound of someone banging and rattling on the door of his room. What did the person want, and what did the gambler do?

Clues: 199/Answer: 261.

LARGE NUMBER

Assume there are approximately five billion people on earth. What would you estimate to be the result, if you multiply together the number of fingers on every person's left hand? (For the purposes of this exercise, thumbs count as fingers, for five fingers per hand.) If you cannot estimate the number, then try to guess how long the number would be.

Clues: 204/Answer: 265.

INNER EAR

An insect flying into a girl's ear terrifies her. Her mother rushes the girl to the doctor, but he is unable to remove the insect. Suddenly, the mother has an idea. What is it?

Clues: 203/Answer: 265.

THE SINGLE FLOWER

A woman was shown into a large room that contained over a thousand flowers. She was told that all but one of the flowers were artificial. She had to identify the real flower, but she could not examine the flowers closely nor smell them. She was alone in the room. What did she do to identify the single flower?

Clues: 207/Answer: 268.

UNSEEN

As far as it is possible to ascertain, there is one thing that only one man in recorded history has not seen. All other men who have sight have seen it. The man was not blind and lived to a ripe old age. What was it that he never saw and why?

Clues: 210/Answer: 270.

THE CHAMPION'S BLIND SPOT

At the dinner to celebrate the end of the Wimbledon tennis championship, the men's singles winner turned to the man next to him and said, "There is something here which you can see and all the other men can see but which I cannot see." What was it?

Clues: 197/Answer: 260.

THE TASK

Several people are waiting to perform a task that they usually do by themselves very easily. Now, however, they are all in need of the services of someone who usually performs the task only with difficulty. What is going on?

Clues: 209/Answer: 270.

WHERE IN THE WORLD?

In what place would you find Julius Caesar, the biblical Rachel, King David, Pallas Athena (the Goddess of War), King Charlemagne, Alexander the Great, Queen Elizabeth I of England, and Sir Lancelot all together?

Clues: 211/Answer: 272.

WALLY TEST V

Just when you thought you were safe—another WALLY test! Write down the answer to each question as soon as possible after reading it. You have just two minutes to complete the test.

1. There were eight ears of corn in a hollow stump. A squirrel can carry out three ears a day. How many days does it take the squirrel to take all the ears of corn from the stump?

2. Which triangle is larger—one with sides measuring 200, 300, and 400 cm or one with sides measuring 300, 400, and 700 cm?

3. How far can a dog run into the woods?

4. Which of the following animals would see best in total darkness: an owl, a leopard, or an eagle?

5. What was the highest mountain in the world before Mount Everest was discovered?

6. Where are the Kings and Queens of England crowned?

7. If the Vice President of the USA were killed, who would then become President?

8. Which candles burn longer—beeswax or tallow?

9. A farmer had four haystacks in one field and twice as many in each of his other two fields. He put the haystacks from all three fields together.

How many haystacks did he now have?

10.   What five-letter word becomes shorter
      when you add two letters to it?

11.   Which weighs more—a pound of feathers or
      a pound of gold?

12.   What has four legs and only one foot?

Answers on page 273.

ORANGE

WHAT A JUMP!

A man jumped 150 feet entirely under his own power. He landed safely. How did he do it?

Clues: 211/Answer: 271.

THE STRING AND THE CLOTH

A man lay dead in a field next to a piece of string and a cloth. How did he die?

Clues: 209/Answer: 269.

A RIDDLE

Four men sat down to play.
They played all night till break of day.
They played for gold and not for fun,
With separate scores for everyone.
When they came to square accounts,
They all made quite fair amounts.
Can you this paradox explain?
If no one lost, how could all gain?

Clues: 207/Answer: 268.

BAD IMPRESSION

A man entered a city art gallery and did terrible damage to some very valuable Impressionist paintings. Later that day, instead of being arrested, he was thanked by the curator of the art gallery for his actions. How come?

Clues: 196/Answer: 259.

THE ANIMAL

At the Carlton Club, Alan Quartermaine was telling one of his stories. "When the animal emerged from the lake I could see that its four knees were wet," he said. Marmaduke, who had walked into the room at that very point, then interrupted, "I know what kind of an animal that was." How did he know, and what kind of animal was it?

Clues: 196/Answer: 259.

THE METAL BALL

At the beginning of his act, a magician places a solid metal ball, four inches in diameter, on a table and places a cover over it. At the end of his act when he lifts the cover, the ball has disappeared. How?

Clues: 205/Answer: 266.

ONE CROAKED!

Two frogs fell into a large cylindrical tank of liquid, and both fell to the bottom. The walls were sheer and slippery. One frog died but one survived. How?

Clues: 206/Answer: 267.

UNSPOKEN UNDERSTANDING

A deaf man went into a subway. He walked up to the cashier's booth and gave the cashier a dollar. The subway tokens cost forty cents each. The cashier gave the man two tokens. Not a word was said, nor any sign given. How did the cashier know that the man indeed wanted two tokens?

Clues: 210/Answer: 271

HIS WIDOW'S SISTER

It was reported in the paper that Jim Jones had married his widow's sister. How did he do this?

Clues: 203/Answer: 264.

LIGHT YEARS AHEAD

If you could travel faster than the speed of light, then you could catch up with the light that radiated from your body some time ago. You would then be able to see yourself as you used to be when you were younger. Although faster-than-light travel is impossible, at least at this time, how can we catch up with the light that we radiated earlier and see ourselves directly—as we used to be? (Such captured images as photographs, movies and videotape do not count.)

Clues: 204/Answer: 266.

THE NEWSPAPER

Jim and Joe were fighting, so their mother punished them by making them both stand on the same sheet of yesterday's newspaper until they were ready to make up. She did this in such a way that neither of the boys could touch the other. How did she manage to do this?

Clues: 205/Answer: 267.

LIGHT WORK

There are three light switches outside a room. They are connected to three light bulbs inside the room. Each switch can be in the "on" position or the "off" position. You are allowed to set the switches and then to enter the room once. You then have to determine which switch is connected to which bulb. How do you do it?

Clues: 204/Answer: 265.

WHAT A BORE!

An office worker has a colleague in her office outstaying his welcome. She can see that he is not inclined to leave any time soon. Concerned about his feelings, how does she manage to get rid of him without offending him?

Clues: 211/Answer: 271.

SOVIET PICTURES

During the dark days of the Soviet Union, purges took place following which experts in photography would doctor photographs to remove individuals who had been purged. How was one expert caught?

Clues: 208/Answer: 269.

PENNILESS

A struggling author receives a present of $2,000 from a lady admirer. He does not tell his wife about this cash gift, although she has shared all his trials and is very supportive. How did she find out that he had received the money?

Clues: 206/Answer: 267.

THE DEADLY SUITCASE

A woman opened a suitcase and found to her horror that there was a body inside. How did it get there?

Clues: 198/Answer: 261.

UNKNOWN CHARACTER

...BUT, MR. SOCKY, YOU ADMIT YOU WERE BLINDED BY A SHOE THE WHOLE TIME...

A recluse who had lived for many years in a small community was charged with a serious crime. He knew nobody in the area. Whom did he call as a character witness?

Clues: 210/Answer: 270.

GASOLINE PROBLEM

A man's car runs out of gasoline. His car tank holds exactly 13 gallons. He has three empty unmarked containers, which can hold

3 gallons, 6 gallons, and 11 gallons. Using only these containers at the gas station, how can the man bring back exactly 13 gallons? He is not allowed to buy more than 13 gallons and dispose of the extra.

Clues: 202/Answer: 264.

POISON PEN

A woman received a very nasty, anonymous letter containing threats and allegations. She called the police and they quickly found out who had sent it. How?

Clues: 206/Answer: 267.

THE COCONUT MILLIONAIRE

A man buys coconuts at $5 a dozen and sells them at $3 a dozen. As a result of this, he becomes a millionaire. How come?

Clues: 198/Answer: 260.

THE MUSIC STOPPED AGAIN

When the music stopped, he died very suddenly. How?

Clues: 205/Answer: 267.

DISREPUTABLE

A man was born before his father, killed his mother, and married his sister. Yet he was considered normal by all those who knew him. How come?

Clues: 198/Answer: 261.

PERSONALITY PLUS

An agency offered personality assessment on the basis of handwriting. How did an enterprising client show that the operation was unreliable?   *Clues: 206/Answer: 267.*

GAMBLER'S RUIN

Syd Sharp, a first-class card player, regularly won large amounts at poker. He was also excellent at bridge, blackjack, cribbage, canasta, and pinochle. Joe, on the other hand, was terrible at cards; he could never remember what had gone before or figure out what card to play next. One day, Joe challenged Syd to a game of cards for money. Over the next couple of hours, Joe proceeded to win quite a large amount from Syd. How?

Clues: 201/Answer: 263.

WALLY TEST VI

Pencils poised? Minds open? Here it is . . . the final WALLY test! Write down the answer to each question as soon as possible after reading it. You have two minutes to complete the test.

1. Which two whole numbers multiplied together make 17?

2. If post is spelled "p-o-s-t" and most is spelled "m-o-s-t," how do you spell the word for what you put in the toaster?

3. What word of five letters contains six when two letters are taken away?

4. A Muslim living in England cannot be buried on church ground even if he converts to Christianity. Why not?

5. How many bananas can a grown man eat on an empty stomach?

6. Why is it that Beethoven never finished the *Unfinished Symphony*?

7. What common word is pronounced wrongly by more than half of all Yale and Harvard graduates?

8. What gets larger the more you take away?

9. If I gave you ten cents for every quarter you could stand on edge and you stood three quarters on their edge, how much money would you gain?

10. If there are 12 six-cent stamps in a dozen, then how many two-cent stamps are there in a dozen?

Answers on page 274.

YELLOW

FAST WORK

When she was picked up, it was discovered that Marion had married 10 men. They were all still alive, but no charges were pressed against her. Why not?

Clues: 199/Answer: 262.

THE FLICKER

A man was running along a corridor clutching a piece of paper. He saw the lights flicker. He gave a cry of anguish and walked on dejectedly. Why?

Clues: 201/Answer: 263.

AN AMERICAN SHOOTING

One American man shot dead another American man in full view of many people. The two men had never met before and did not know each other. Neither was a policeman nor a criminal. The man who shot and killed the other man was not arrested or charged with any crime. Why not?

Clues: 196/Answer: 259.

KING GEORGE

King George the Third of England suffered a temporary bout of madness. A movie was made in England on this subject. It was entitled "The Madness of George III," but this name was changed for American audiences. Why?

Clues: 203/Answer: 265.

FALLEN ANGEL

A butterfly fell down, and a man was seriously injured. Why?

Clues: 199/Answer: 262.

THE FLAW IN THE CARPET

A man bought a very expensive oriental carpet in a reputable carpet shop in a Middle Eastern country. After he had bought it, he found that it had a flaw. He took it back to the shop. It was agreed that there was a flaw in the carpet, but the shopkeeper refused to take back the carpet or give any kind of refund or reduction in price. Why not?

Clues: 201/Answer: 263.

WHAT A RELIEF!

Immediately after the end of World War II, a doctor in France approached a soldier who was perfectly healthy and asked for a large sample of his urine. Why was this?

Clues: 211/Answer: 271.

FIRST CHOICE

A travel article on Brazil observed that, in restaurants in Rio, soup was a very popular starter choice for rich ladies. Why?

Clues: 200/Answer: 262.

DISTURBANCE

A man went to his neighbor's house at three in the morning and started shouting and banging on the door. He would not stop until the neighbors opened the door and stood facing him. Initially angry, they later thanked the man. Why?

Clues: 198/Answer: 261.

MONA LISA

Why did a group of enterprising thieves steal the famous painting the Mona Lisa and then return it undamaged a few months later?

Clues: 205/Answer: 266.

SNOW JOY

Children in a town in New England were delighted one snowy January day. The snow was so heavy that school had to be canceled. Their joy continued when the deep snow caused the same thing to happen on the next few days. Then they became disappointed and upset at having to miss school. Why?

Clues: 208/Answer: 269.

FIREWORKS DISPLAY

A young family went out to a fireworks display. On their return, the parents were very sad. Why?

Clues: 200/Answer: 262.

THE FALLEN GUIDE

A mountain climber in the Himalayas took along with him two mountain guides. After a few hours, one of the guides fell into a deep crevasse. The climber and the other guide continued the climb and did not raise the alarm. Why?

Clues: 199/Answer: 262.

THE YACHT INCIDENT

A yacht is found floating in the middle of the ocean, and around it in the water are a dozen human corpses. Why?

Clues: 212/Answer: 272.

SELF-ADDRESSED ENVELOPE

Why does a man send himself a letter every day but Saturday?

Clues: 207/Answer: 268.

FINGERED

Why did a political candidate always place his finger on the chest of any man when he was canvassing people in public?

Clues: 200/Answer: 262.

THE GROSS GROCERY LIST

A woman handed a man a grocery list, but when he handed it back to her she was extremely embarrassed. Why?

Clues: 202/Answer: 264.

FINGER BREAK

Why did a woman take a baseball bat and break her husband's fingers?

Clues: 200/Answer: 262.

UNPUBLISHED

An eminent firm of publishers had a manuscript for a novel. It was written by a very well known author and was sure to sell well. However, they chose not to publish it. Why?

Clues: 210/Answer: 270.

THE WOUNDED SOLDIER

A badly wounded but conscious soldier is brought into a field hospital during a battle. The surgeon takes a quick look at him and then says to the orderly, "Get this man out of here! He is a coward who has smeared himself with the blood of his comrades." Why does he say this?

Clues: 212/Answer: 272

THE UNWANTED GIFT

A nobleman was very displeased when he received an expensive gift from the King. Why?

Clues: 210/Answer: 271.

BENJAMIN FRANKLIN

Benjamin Franklin was a well-educated man. Why did he spell "Philadelphia" deliberately wrong?

Clues: 196/Answer: 259.

MIDDLE EASTERN MUDDLE

One of the most successful advertising agencies in the USA acquired a Middle Eastern account. Their first ad there made them a laughingstock. Why?

Clues: 205/Answer: 266.

ICE RINKED

A man skating at an ice rink saw a woman slip and fall. Although she was a stranger to him, he wanted to find out if she was all right. He went over to her, but before he said anything, she slapped him hard across the face. They had never met or communicated before. Why did she strike him?

Clues: 203/Answer: 265.

ON TIME

Why did a man who knew the time and had two accurate watches phone the speaking clock?

Clues: 206/Answer: 267.

CAT FOOD

A man who did not like cats bought some fresh salmon and cream for a cat. Why?

Clues: 197/Answer: 260.

RICH MAN, POOR MAN

A man making more than $10 million a year drives a small car, lives in a modest house, and insists he can't afford luxuries. Why not?

Clues: 207/Answer: 268.

SLEEPING ON THE JOB

A man undressed to go to bed and hundreds of people lost their jobs. Why?

Clues: 208/Answer: 268.

FINE ART

An art collector went into the art dealer, Sotheby's. He asked to have two items valued. One was an old violin and the other, an oil painting. The experts studied them for days before confirming their remarkable findings. The collector was told that the two items were an original Stradivarius and a previously unknown work by Vincent van Gogh. At first, the collector was thrilled, but later he became very dejected. Why?

Clues: 200/Answer: 262.

FORD'S LUNCH

Before hiring anyone in a senior post, Henry Ford, the auto magnate, always took the candidate out to dinner. Why?

Clues: 201/Answer: 263.

FRUITLESS SEARCH

A man was searching for blue-back frogs in an area where they were very common. He caught one. It started to rain, and he became frantic. The rain grew stronger, and the man left, disconsolate. Why?

Clues: 201/Answer: 263.

CHECKED

A man wrote out and signed a check from his own checkbook for $1,000. There was more than this in his account. Yet he was charged with fraud. Why?

Clues: 198/Answer: 260.

THESE PUZZLES

You have certainly noticed that the puzzles in this book are divided into three color categories. This was done for a reason that by now should be more or less apparent to you. This puzzle also fits the mold. So, why have the puzzles been placed in their particular categories?

Clues: 209/Answer: 270.

THE CHEAT

A man cheated a woman out of a sum of $5. When she found out, she killed him. They were not poor. Her defense lawyer argued that she was justified in her actions, and many people agreed with her. Why?

Clues: 197/Answer: 260.

DUTCH RACE

One of the most prestigious races in Holland involves many people and enormous organization. But nobody knows when it will be held until two days before the race. Why?

Clues: 199/Answer: 261.

WHOOPS!

A man was enjoying his meal at a dinner party and had just started a delicious dessert. Why did he deliberately knock over the salt cellar into his dessert and ruin it?

Clues: 211/Answer: 272.

GARDEN STORY

Why did a man tell his wife that he had buried guns in their garden when he knew that he had not?

Clues: 202/Answer: 264.

CLUES TO
PERPLEXING PUZZLES

⌒ **An American Shooting**

Although an innocent man was killed,
  no crime was committed.

Both men were armed.

This took place in the nineteenth century.

⌒ **The Animal**

Marmaduke was able to deduce what the animal was from
  Alan Quartermaine's statement alone.

Only one animal has just four knees.

⌒ **Bad Impression**

He deliberately sprayed water over the paintings. This
  damaged them.

He was not unstable, deranged or malevolent. He acted out
  of good intentions.

⌒ **Benjamin Franklin**

Benjamin Franklin deliberately spelled Philadelphia wrong
  as part of his job. He was not involved in teaching.

He was trying to make things more difficult for those who
made his job difficult.

∾ Buttons

This is not a fashion issue. It has to do with right-
and left-handedness.

When buttons first came into use, it was the better-off
who used them.

∾ Cat Food

He wanted the cat to do something for him.

∾ The Champion's Blind Spot

The winner had perfect eyesight and could see
as well as any other person there but, nonetheless, others
could see something he could not see.

He could not see something relative to him that others
could see relative to them.

If the winner had lost a game, then he could not make
this claim.

∾ The Cheat

The man had failed to keep a promise.

He had not used the $5 as agreed.

The woman found herself considerably worse off
than she had expected.

∿ Checked

His signature was perfect.

He intended to defraud. The check looked fine, but it would not have proven valid.

∿ The Coconut Millionaire

He lost money on every coconut he sold.

He did not make money by any related activity.

∿ Color-Blind

He was employed by the military.

He could see things other people found difficult to see.

∿ The Deadly Suitcase

The body was that of a child who had died accidentally through suffocation.

The woman was poor and had tried to save money.

∿ Disreputable

This is really three puzzles in one.

He was born after his father was. He did not murder his mother. He did not commit incest.

∿ Disturbance

He was trying to warn them.

They were not in danger, but he thought they were.

∿ Dutch Race

The race can only take place under certain conditions.
These conditions occur infrequently.

∿ Early Morning in Las Vegas

The person who banged on the door was not a hotel official,
nor a police officer or other such authority.

The gambler was not in danger.

∿ Fallen Angel

The butterfly was not a live butterfly.

The man walked into trouble.

The model butterfly served as a warning.

∿ The Fallen Guide

The first guide fell into the deep ravine and was lost from
view. Both the climber and the second guide were fit and
healthy. They had time to try to rescue the first guide,
but they did not bother.

The climber believed that the first guide was not important
to him and could be replaced.

∿ Fast Work

Marion had committed no crime.

She was single.

∾ Fine Art

The art collector learned that his two very valuable works were worth far less than he had assumed.

There was no mistake. Sotheby's correctly identified the works.

∾ Finger Break

She had good intentions.
He was in danger.

∾ Fingered

He was vain.
He wanted maximum publicity.

∾ Fireworks Display

The family consisted of two parents, their four-year-old daughter, and their two-month-old son.

The fireworks display went perfectly. There were no accidents or injuries. The children enjoyed it.

The parents learned something.

∾ First Choice

This had nothing to do with taste, nutrition, diet, or food.

There was a practical reason why rich ladies preferred soup in restaurants. It did not apply at home.

∾ The Flaw in the Carpet

The shop explained that, although there was a flaw
  in the carpet, it was not the result of an error or mistake.

The carpet makers were devout Muslims.

∾ The Flicker

He knew that someone had died.

The piece of paper could have saved a life.

∾ Ford's Lunch

Henry Ford was giving the person a form of test, although
  the candidate for the position did not realize it.

He watched carefully as the candidate consumed his soup.

∾ Fruitless Search

Blue-back frogs are now extinct.

The man was very religious.

He wanted to get back to his boat.

∾ Gambler's Ruin

They played cards, but Joe chose a game that suited him
  better than it suited Syd.

Syd had a handicap at this particular child's game.

∿ Garden Story

The man had lied, but not with the intention of deceiving his wife.

He was worried that the hard work of gardening would be a strain for his wife, who lived alone and had no one to help her.

∿ Gasoline Problem

No complex mathematical combinations are needed to solve this one.

∿ Gertrude

Gertrude caused a mechanical failure in the plane.

It was a jet aircraft.

∿ The Gross Grocery List

The grocery list contained nothing more than a list of regular and ordinary groceries.

The man to whom she handed the list was not a grocer.

She had set out that morning with two lists.

∿ The Hammer

Adam did not use the hammer on the computer. computer was undamaged.

Brenda had a disability.

∾ His Widow's Sister

When Jim Jones died, his wife became a widow.

No bigamy is involved and no life after death.

He had married his widow's sister quite legitimately.

∾ Ice Rinked

She misunderstood his intentions.

Although he did not say a word,
    he did try to communicate with her.

∾ Inner Ear

The mother lures the insect out of her daughter's ear.

∾ King George

It was decided that the title might mislead audiences.

∾ The King's Favor

In a way, the King got what he wanted, and the College
    got what it wanted.

The King took the portrait along with him when he
    left Cambridge.

No copy was made.

∾ The Late Report

The man was not involved in any way in the death of the
    person whose body he had reported.

The man had not noticed the body earlier, but did later.

Large Number

The answer can be quickly and accurately deduced.

Think about the effect of actually multiplying the number of fingers on the left hands of all the people in the world, one after another.

The calculation might start

$5 \times 5 \times 5 \times 5 \times 5 \times 5 \times 5 \times 5 \times 4 \times 5 \times 5 \times 5 \times 5 \times$ ... and so on.

Light Work

With just two bulbs and two switches, it would be easy.

Light bulbs give out light. What else do they do when they are switched on?

Light Years Ahead

There is a way in which we can see the light that we radiated and therefore an image of the way we were.

It is a common experience to view this image.

Mad Cow Ideas

The Cambodian government suggested a way for Britain to get rid of the suspect cattle without risking that the cattle would eventually be eaten.

The suggestion involved the eventual death of the cattle in a way that would help solve a Cambodian problem.

∿ The Metal Ball

The magician need not do anything to make the ball vanish.
He carefully makes and stores the ball before his act.

∿ Middle Eastern Muddle

They produced an ad, which was misunderstood.
Their ad had no words.

∿ Mona Lisa

They did it for money.

No insurance payment was involved.
The thieves did not receive any reward or payment from the police, museum, insurance company, or any public body.

∿ The Music Stopped Again

This has nothing to do with tightrope walkers!
A game was taking place. It involved music.

∿ The Newspaper

Jim and Joe were normal boys, aged seven and eight.
They both stood on the same sheet of newspaper but, try as they might, they could not touch or even see each other without leaving the newspaper.

∿ On Time

He was not interested in the time.

He wanted to make an innocuous telephone call.

He was cheating.

∿ One Croaked!

The frogs were physically identical. One managed to survive the ordeal because of the result of its actions.

The nature of the liquid is important.

∿ Penniless

The author did not know the identity of the lady admirer.

His wife was not jealous or concerned about the gift.

∿ Personality Plus

The client submitted handwriting tests. He then simply showed that the assessments were incorrect.

∿ Poison Pen

They examined the letter very carefully.

The letter came from a pad of writing paper.

∿ Price Tag

A price set at five cents, or even one cent, under a round dollar amount means that a customer would be entitled to change from a bill.

Smart shopkeepers were trying to protect themselves
from losses.

∾ Rich Man, Poor Man

The man makes more than $10 million a year at his work,
but he does not have a lot to spend.

He is not wealthy, nor does he have any major debts
or expenses.

∾ A Riddle

They played seriously and each did his best.

Each man came out ahead.

No one joined their group.

∾ Seaside Idea

He was a senior officer in the Royal Air Force.

He and his children threw stones into the sea.

∾ Self-Addressed Envelope

He posts a letter so that he will receive a letter.

He wants to be sure of seeing the postman
on every possible delivery.

∾ The Single Flower

She got some help.

No other person was involved.

∿ Sleeping on the Job

The man was a movie star.

The people who lost their jobs worked
in the garment industry.

∿ Snow Joy

Naturally, the children would much rather be at home,
or out playing, than go to school.

There was nothing special going on at school to attract
the children back.

There was a consequence of an extended school cancellation,
which they did not want.

∿ Souper

She was perfectly capable of consuming the soup
with a spoon. There was nothing wrong with the soup.

Something happened halfway through the course that
caused her to want to use the straw.

∿ Soviet Pictures

A fault was found in the photograph,
which proved it had been tampered with.

A fault was discovered by a Count.

∿ The Stranger in the Bar

The two men were drinking beer while the stranger
was drinking soda water.

The two men hadn't noticed the stranger outside the bars,
>   but there was a connection between them
>   and the stranger.

∿ The Stranger in the Hotel

Hers was a single room.

There was nothing unusual about the man's appearance
>   or bearing. The woman made a deduction based
>   on what he said.

∿ The String and the Cloth

He died an accidental death.

He had been holding the string.

It was a windy day.

∿ The Task

The person who is performing the task has a disability.

Circumstances have changed so that the person's disability
>   gives him an advantage over the others.

∿ These Puzzles

Each puzzle belongs to one and only one section,
>   based on a single characteristic of the words
>   of the puzzle.

The categories could have been called A, O, and Y—
>   but that is not as colorful!

Each puzzle is a question.

∿ Unknown Character

He called someone who did not know him.

By calling this person he hoped to prove that he
was not a bad character.

∿ Unpublished

The publication of the novel would not cause offense
or any legal actions.

The title of the novel was well known.

∿ Unseen

It is known that this man led a secluded life.

Other men, even those blind from birth, would hear and
touch this thing, but this man never heard or touched it.

∿ Unspoken Understanding

The man did want two tokens, and the cashier
was able to correctly deduce this.

Nothing was written or signaled.

∿ The Unwanted Gift

The gift was costly to maintain.

The gift was of a rare color.

∿ Upstairs, Downstairs

The restaurant is in an unusual location.

∾ **What a Bore!**

The woman arranges an interruption,
   but no one else is involved.

She enjoys the advantages of modern technology.

∾ **What a Jump!**

He was an athlete.

He did not use any extra source of power
   but did use special equipment.

This happens regularly in a certain sporting event.

∾ **What a Relief!**

The soldier's urine contained something of use
   to the doctor.

The soldier was an American GI.

This was a common practice among many French doctors.

∾ **Where in the World?**

Their images are found together in one common place.

They are found on something which is in common use
   and has been for many years.

They are used in a form of game.

∾ **Whoops!**

He did not want to eat the dessert,
   but didn't want to appear rude.

He was hungry, normally enjoyed this dessert, and had
   started it with gusto. It had tasted good, and he felt fine.

∿ **The Wounded Soldier**

The soldier was genuinely wounded and was not a coward. The doctor knew this.

The doctor lied, but had good intentions and wanted to help the soldier.

∿ **The Yacht Incident**

They had been passengers aboard the yacht.

They died because of an accident. They drowned.

ANSWERS

CLEVER PUZZLES

Arrested Anyway (page 6)—Rocky took one airplane to an intermediate stop, got out, and got into a second airplane to his final destination. If he had told the airline that he was doing so, then his fare would have been higher. He was trying to save money by noting that the fares for the separate parts of his trip were less than the equivalent fare for the whole trip. Therefore, he could not check the suitcase directly to the final destination, but had to retrieve it and re-check it at the intermediate stop. Rocky did not have a firearm permit for the state in which he made the intermediate stop, but was carrying the gun. He was arrested for that reason.

Burning Down the Building (page 4)—The landlord set fire to his own building. It was occupied by tenants who paid a low rent that was restricted by law. If they moved out, then he would have vacant apartments that could be offered at a much higher rent than before. Incurring fire damage was a sensible investment, for it would remove the low-rent tenants and permit elegant remodeling into luxury apartments that could fetch a very high rent.

Caught in the Act (page 5)—In this true story, a neighborhood pickpocket was caught by a woman, the wife of eighteenth-century inventor Peter Cooper, who sewed fishhooks into her coat pocket. When he caught his hand on the hooks, she told him, "I am going to the police station, and you are coming with me." He cooperated to prevent serious injury to his hand.

Contagious Carsickness? (page 11)—Stan had, as he had planned, stopped the car on a ferry boat. Jan became seasick.

Dots on the I's (page 23)—A small I has one dot over it. A small I with a dot over it, therefore, actually has two dots, one above the other. Timmy took a pen and put two dots on his forehead, one over each eye.

Driving the Wrong Car (page 8)—The battery on the broken car was dead, and Hermie knew that the electrical system was suspect. He wanted the car checked thoroughly. He jump-started it with the working car, after which it could be driven. The working car had a manual transmission and could be towed without transmission damage. But the jump-started car had an automatic transmission, which is affected by towing. Hermie, therefore, towed the car that had the manual transmission.

Easy Money (page 31)—Butch stole the TV sets from his employer, making a profit of $30 for each set that he sold.

The Empty Wrapper (page 18)—She had her two-year-old son with her. When her son got hungry, she got permission from a store manager to buy a sandwich at the delicatessen counter, give it to her son, and pay for it later at the checkout counter with the rest of her merchandise.

The Fast Elevator Trip (page 15)—When the elevator arrived, other people crowded into it; Bill critically watched them push buttons for several floors. Bill figured that the elevator would stop at the most floors at which it could stop. Therefore, noting that another elevator was approaching, he decided to get onto it instead; for he would share it with fewer passengers while it made far fewer intermediate stops on the way to his appointment. Avoiding the intermediate stops was worth the wait.

Forgot to Stop? (page 19)—The car ran off a bridge and fell into a lake, and Angus jumped out just as the car hit its surface.

Gas-Station Glitch (page 31)—The man whom George paid was not an employee of the station, but a con artist who got a uniform, asked everyone in line for ten dollars, and left quickly.

Giving Wayne the Boot (page 16)—Burglars had cut the neighbor's telephone wire and broken into his house. In self-defense, he barricaded himself into an upstairs room and successfully provoked Wayne to call the police.

Happy with the TV Ad (page 25)—The man was a political candidate running for a local office. Tipped off that his rival had bought a 30-minute infomercial time slot, he bought the minute just before it and broadcast a test pattern, hoping to induce TV viewers not to continue watching that particular channel.

He Called the Police (page 7)—Once inside the house, he fell, breaking his leg. Pulling a telephone down from a table, he called an emergency police number for help and, though arrested, received treatment for his leg.

I've Got Your Number (page 20)—Kingfist found the telephone wiring that led into Sam's house and put one pin into each wire. Then he connected a telephone to the pins and dialed a long-distance number that was sure to answer, carefully charging the call on a telephone calling card. A few days later, he called his long-distance carrier and asked about possible misuse of the card and named the number that he had called. He easily learned the number that he had called from.

Inefficiency Pays Off (page 29)—An air conditioner. The models with the most cooling power have stronger motors and cost more than those with less power. But because they cool air substantially, only a small fraction of the air in a room needs to pass through the mechanism to cool a room by a specified amount. Most of the air in the room does not pass through the air conditioner as the room gets cool. What does pass through it is sufficiently cold to cool the entire room. But as temperature goes down, relative humidity goes up. The dissolved moisture in most of the air is not removed, and a too-strong air conditioner makes a room feel not only cool but also damp.

The Late Train (page 11)—During the night, which was the last Saturday in March, the time was advanced from standard time to daylight-saving time. The engineer gained fifteen minutes during the night, but the train was still late when Amanda got off it.

Long-Life Bulbs (page 24)—Modern incandescent bulbs have a coiled filament that glows as current is passed through it. A coil, however, radiates and absorbs magnetic impulses as the current through it is changed. It thereby not only resists changes in current (the electrical equivalent of inertia), but also shakes slightly as the voltage changes. The voltage changes with alternating current between +166 volts and −166 volts and back again 60 times per second, placing mechanical stress on the filament. Eric merely used direct current, so that the filaments would not be shaken by voltage changes and would last longer for that reason.

Magazine Subscriptions (page 22)—Postage for a first-class item with a reply-paid address must be paid by the recipient. City residents may hoard the cards in case of a garbage collectors' strike, perhaps believing that those who contribute to the garbage problem should help solve it at their own expense.

Making the Grade (page 13)—Nell could not hand in a postcard with her term paper because, although the paper was not due for another week, she had already handed it in. She was then free to write other term papers and study for exams in other courses.

The Mail Is In! (page 21)—Oscar knew the procedure for receiving a package by mail. You take the key from your mailbox, unlock the pod, and take the package from the pod. The key stays in the pod door. Only a mail carrier can remove a key from a pod door. When Oscar saw a pod without a key and remembered that the pod had had a key on the previous day, he knew that the mail carrier had delivered the day's mail.

The Mirror (page 17)—It is one of two mirrors, both made of special optical-grade glass to prevent eyestrain. The mirror that is not over the headboard is mounted, on a flexible bracket, near it. After adjusting the second mirror, one can lie on one's back and look in it and see the reflection from the first mirror. By looking through two mirrors, one sees an unreversed image. This arrangement is useful for someone with a bad back who wants to lie in bed and watch TV, for one need not be propped up but can lie truly flat.

More Short-Lived Writing (page 19)—Erasing colored chalk from a blackboard. Yolanda is a teacher and sometimes draws diagrams on the blackboard using different colors of chalk. Erasing such diagrams leaves colored smudges on the blackboard. Yolanda discovered that scribbling over the colored smudges with white chalk and then erasing the scribbling helps to remove the colored smudges and, unlike wiping the blackboard with a wet rag, permits immediate re-use of it.

A Mystery Fax (page 14)—Quietly interested in changing jobs, the executive arranged for a cooperative recruiter to try to fax him a blank sheet of paper when trying to reach him. If he could talk, then he announced himself over the fax signal. If not, he called the recruiter later when he could discreetly do so.

No TV Trouble (page 28)—A pocket-size TV set was on top of the dashboard, and it was off. Stuart was listening to an audio-cassette with his favorite show's theme music.

The Nonstop Elevator Trip (page 12)—The floor was at the top of one range of floors served by one group of elevators. Jill instead used the adjacent group of elevators, going to the lowest floor served by them, which was one floor above her floor. Then, after her nonstop elevator ride, she merely walked down one flight of stairs.

Not from the USA (page 22)—Windsor, Canada, adjacent to Detroit, Michigan, is directly both south and east of parts of Michigan. It is north and west of other USA states.

Picture the Tourists (page 17)—Sal's camera focused by measuring the distance to the object in front of it, which would be the window of the bus. Sal's pictures of objects outside the bus would, therefore, be badly out of focus. But autofocus does not work when the distance is very small. Sherman wanted Sal to sit close to the window, so that the camera would ignore it and focus for great distance and would take good pictures.

Power Failure (page 23)—Power failures occurred often. Horace, therefore, did not bother resetting clocks every time the power was restored. When the power failed during the night, the clocks had not been reset from the previous power failure and looked unchanged in the morning.

Racing the Drawbridge (page 16)—Clarence was navigating a boat, and the drawbridge was opened to let it pass.

Safe Smash-Up (page 10)—No one was in the car. It had been parked on a hill, and the driver who parked it forgot to set the brakes. Since the ignition was not on, there was no spark or other flame source to set fire to the fuel.

Scared of Her Shadow? (page 17)—She drives an old car, with taillight lenses that have not been cleaned from the inside for perhaps ten years. Sunlight shining on taillight lenses can make brake and turn signals nearly impossible to see, particularly with dirty lenses or the dim bulbs in very old cars. Hand signals, under those circumstances, are more easily seen. Florida law permits hand signals for sufficiently small cars, even if the taillights work.

Secret Business (page 30)—The men were planning a big business deal, and they were pretty sure that their telephones were tapped. They used a simple scrambler that could easily be obtained by an eavesdropper. But before the telephone conversation, they wrote a script for a fake conversation in which they discussed doing the opposite of what they really planned to do. They wanted eavesdroppers to anticipate the wrong plans and lose money, which the two men would gain. A secure scrambler would not have allowed eavesdroppers to hear the staged conversation and would not have helped the two men.

Secret Fuel (page 19)—Marvin's neighbor had recently bought an extravagant sports car and bragged about it constantly. Hoping to quiet him down, Marvin poured a gallon of fuel into its fuel tank every few nights. After the neighbor began to boast about his new car's outstanding mileage, Marvin knew that his plan would work: merely add fuel quietly, then stop and let the neighbor wonder why the mileage suddenly deteriorated just as the warranty expired.

She Arrived On Time (page 9)—Carol was not at home. She had had her telephone calls diverted to her cellular phone and simply happened to be in the coffee house when Daryl called her.

Short-Lived Messages (page 19)—Yolanda has an IBM-compatible computer and an Apple computer and wants to transmit data between them. With only one modem and little technical knowledge, she sends the data to herself through an on-line electronic-mail service with one computer and receives the data with the other computer.

Smashed Taillights (page 4)—Bob had been kidnapped and locked in a car trunk. Aware of police department recommendations, he fumbled for the tire wrench and, having loosened it from its storage brackets, broke the taillights and side markers from inside. Then he was able to wave the wrench to passersby and to call for help.

Soliciting in Seattle (page 22)—In Seattle, one building houses the headquarters of several charity canvassing organizations. They send workers out to collect money, and those workers usually walk from the building when they start canvassing and return to it on foot when they are finished. Only one of the friends' two houses was within easy walking distance of that building.

Staged Roulette (page 31)—The police chief had a crooked gambling joint raided and easily obtained a rigged roulette wheel for the show.

Strange Sounds (page 27)—Some movies in the 1980s had scenes in which someone was typing, but the sounds of the keys were unrelated to the motion of the typist's fingers. Nowadays, scenes of typing conceal the hands to prevent that error. Reverberations remain a clue, as when a person walks from the out-doors into a narrow corridor and the footsteps do not reverberate indoors. Another clue is the absence of a companion sound, as when several people are walking and only one set of footsteps is heard. Or when a horse-drawn cart is shown and horses' hoofs are heard—but the cartwheels themselves are totally silent.

Stubborn Steve (page 12)—Steve was going to use the paper in airmail letters to correspondents overseas. To save postage, he wanted paper as light as possible, even if it was expensive and occasionally jammed his printer.

Supposed to Kill? (page 4)—A scene was being filmed for a movie. For the protection of actors, it was universally agreed that anyone on the receiving end of a firearm had to load it personally with nonhazardous "blanks." This particular actor had forgotten to load the gun, and the scene had to be refilmed.

They Had a Ball (page 24)—The two men were not alone. Ted saw a teammate behind Ned and feared that if Ned missed the high ball, then the teammate might be hit by it. A throw directly to someone's body was different, for it would at least be deflected if it was missed. Ted aimed his high throw so that if Ned missed the ball, it would not hit anyone.

Time for Repairs (page 26)—When he first looked at his watch in the morning, it showed the time 10:01. Later that morning, it showed 11:11. During his lunch break, it showed 12:21. The rest of the morning, it did not show the correct time. Dilton was unknowingly wearing his digital watch upside down.

A Token Wait in a Token Line (page 8)—Smart Stephanie observed that most commuters bought tokens as they entered the subway from the street. She merely bought tokens as she left the subway, when few other commuters did so.

The TV Obeyed (page 28)—Eager to show off his elaborate new equipment, Jake had friends over. Not only did he set up his videocassette player, but also he carefully reviewed the instructions for his TV set, which included a timer that would turn it off a specified time later. He carefully set the shutoff timer to outlast the movie by a minute or two and, when the ad came on, saw a warning on the screen that the TV would turn itself off in a couple of seconds. He knew that it would be shutting off immediately, so he shouted at the TV set just for the fun of it.

Watching the Game (page 26)—Satellite signals are generally scrambled. To receive them in usable form, you buy an electronic device (a transponder) and pay royalties to the satellite company, which in turn sets your transponder to unscramble the appropriate signals. Elmer's accomplice ran a sports bar in a distant city and also had a transponder. To obtain unscrambled signals of locally blacked-out games, they merely swapped transponders.

Welcome, Slasher (page 3)—A hurricane emergency had been declared, and poorly constructed buildings were at risk of major structural damage. Screens imposed wind resistance, which could stress buildings enough to wreck them. Removing screens from screened porches was correctly announced as a safety measure, even if the screens were permanently stapled in place, so the boy had an opportunity to divert his destructive tendencies to a good cause. The policeman knew that the frantic absent homeowners had requested the boy's help with this potential problem.

What Drained the Battery? (page 10)—Walter, in a rush, forgot to turn off the headlights. No one else entered the parking lot until lunchtime, when managers customarily went out to eat. One of them turned off Walter's headlights, although by then the battery didn't have enough power to start the engine.

Youthful Gamble (page 30)—College students, despite uniform room charges, are often assigned dormitory rooms of unequal sizes by lottery. Similarly, equal tuition payments do not necessarily result in equal education, because lotteries are used to select which students get access to popular courses that have enrollment quotas.

TRICKY PUZZLES

Another Landlubber (page 60)—He was an astronaut in a space ship.

Bertha's Travels (page 55)—Bertha is an elevator operator.

Blow by Blow (page 67)—The assistant at the fairground blew darts through a concealed blowpipe to burst the balloons of children on their way home from the fair so that their parents would have to return to buy replacement balloons to stem the tears.

Bus-Lane Bonus (page 67)—Emergency vehicles and, in particular, ambulances were allowed to use the bus lanes. Ambulances reached accident victims sooner and got them to the hospital sooner so fewer of them died.

Cheap and Cheerful (page 80)—The food is salmon. Previously he had choked on a bone in fresh salmon. The salt in canned salmon dissolves the bones and removes this danger.

Chop Chop (page 63)—For a short time on sunny days, the shadow of the old tree covered an instrument used for recording sunshine. The instrument had been put in place on a cloudy day. Good sense prevailed and the instrument was moved instead.

Co-Lateral Damage (page 72)—They strengthened the parts of the aircraft that had not been hit. Anti-aircraft fire is random in nature. The returning planes showed damage that had not been fatal. But this sample excludes information from the planes that had not returned and had sustained fatal damage. It was deduced that they had sustained damage on the parts not hit on the returning planes. By adding armor to the planes, overall losses were reduced.

The Costly Wave (page 74)—The man was the winner of the prestigious London Marathon race. He waved to the large crowd the entire way down the finishing straightaway and, because of that, he just failed to break the record time for the marathon—thereby missing out on the $30,000 bonus prize.

Criminal Assistance (page 56)—The police put up notices "Beware of Pickpockets." The pickpockets stood near a sign and noticed that when people saw it they immediately checked that their purses and wallets were safe. The pickpockets then knew where their victims carried their purses and wallets—which made them easier to steal.

The Deadly Dresser (page 59)—The last thing he put on was his shoe. It contained a deadly spider that bit him, and he died soon after.

The Deadly Feather (page 85)—The man was a circus sword swallower. In the middle of his act someone tickled him with the feather, and he gagged.

The Deadly Omelet (page 77)—The man was an aristocrat on the run from the French Revolution. He disguised himself as a peasant. When he ordered an omelet, he was asked how many eggs he wanted in it. He replied, "A dozen." No peasant would have asked for more than two or three.

The Deadly Stone (page 74)—The man was lost in the desert. Without landmarks, he marked stones with a drop of blood from a cut on his hand. After two days of walking and out of water, he found a stone with blood on it. He knew that he was walking in circles, and he shot himself rather than face a slower death.

Denise and Harry (page 58)—Denise and Harry were hurricanes.

The Dinner Clue (page 76)—The meal included a large piece of stale cheese that the suspect bit into and then left. His teeth marks were found to match a bite on the body of a murder victim.

Disconnected? (page 72)—The horse worked in a mill. It walked around in a circle all day to drive the millstone. In the course of the day, its outer legs walked a mile farther than its inner legs.

Eensy Weensy Spider Farm (page 78)—Spiderwebs are bought by unscrupulous wine merchants who want to give the impression that their wines are old and mature.

The Engraving (page 62)—She received a used British postage stamp.

Face-off (page 79)—The French tested their artillery by firing some shots into the mountains. This caused avalanches that killed many soldiers on both sides.

Floating Home (page 71)—The man was an astronaut.

Foreign Cure (page 65)—The man is an alcoholic. He flies to a country where alcohol is banned by law in the hope of curing his addiction by removing the temptation.

Forging Ahead (page 68)—The forger bought a cheap item with the genuine $50 bill. In the change he would usually get at least one $20 bill. He would then ask the storekeeper to change the $20 bill into two tens and switch the genuine $20 bill with a forged one of his own making. The storekeeper was less likely to check a bill he believed he had just paid out.

Frozen Assets (page 82)—During World War II, the Russians built a railway line over the frozen Lake Ladoga to deliver supplies to the city of Leningrad, which was under siege from German forces. Its population was starving, and there was no means of supply from the Russian side other than over the lake.

The Gap (page 76)—The man was carving a tombstone. A husband had died and the man carved:

PRAY FOR HI M.

When the wife died, she would be buried with her husband, and the engraving would be amended to:

PRAY FOR THEM.

Half for Me and Half for You (page 61)—Lucrezia Borgia put a deadly poison on one side of the blade of a knife. When she cut the apple, only one half was poisoned.

Hearty Appetite (page 70)—After the Exxon Valdez oil spill, an enormous amount of money was spent cleansing the environment and rehabilitating oil-damaged animals. Two seals had been carefully nurtured back to good health at a cost of more than $100,000, and they were released into the sea in front of an appreciative crowd. A few minutes later, the crowd was horrified to see them both eaten by a killer whale.

High on a Hill (page 69)—The man was marooned on a volcano that had recently erupted. He was kept alive by the heat of the melting lava.

History Question (page 68)—Absolutely nothing happened in London on September 8, 1752. It was one of the eleven days dropped when the old calendar was adjusted to the new one.

Honorable Intent (page 57)—The six people had all received different organs from a donor who had died in an accident. They meet to honor his memory.

Hot Job (page 63)—The man wore a short-sleeved shirt, and his name was tattooed on his arm.

Inheritance (page 81)—The younger son took his sword and cut off his hand before hurling it ashore. Since he had touched the shore before his brother, he was able to claim his father's kingdom.

(This story is told of the kingdom of Ulster, and to this day a bloody red hand is used as the symbol of the province.)

In the Middle of the Night (page 56)—He turns on the light.

Jericho (page 61)—The man was building a house of cards.

Joker (page 73)—When one player went to play a card, she knocked over a mug. The hot drink poured over the other player, who immediately jumped up and started to take her clothes off.

Landlubber (page 59)—He sailed around the coast of Antarctica.

The Last Mail (page 84)—Both letters were the same weight, a fraction under the weight at which a surcharge was charged. He put the correct postage amount in stamps on each letter. One had a single stamp of the correct value, and the other had several stamps adding up to the correct value. When the letters were weighed, the one with the more stamps was over the limit, and so more stamps were needed.

Lethal Relief (page 62)—The food was dropped by parachute in remote areas. Several people were killed when the packages fell on them.

Lifesaver (page 59)—The politician was Teddy Roosevelt, the American president. In 1912, in Milwaukee, he was shot in the chest. He was saved because the bullet was slowed as it passed through the folded manuscript of the speech in his breast pocket. He went on to make the speech later on the same day that he was shot!

The Man Who Did Not Fly (page 81)—In this true case, many vacationers who flew with a certain airline had their homes burglarized while they were away. The police added a false name (but real address) to the list and caught the burglar red-handed when he broke in. It turned out that his sister worked for the airline and passed the list of passenger addresses to her nefarious brother.

The Man Who Would Not Read (page 78)—He saw a notice on the side of the carriage that said, "This carriage is not for Reading." Reading is a town on the main line between London and Bristol.

Material Witness (page 58)—They are on the window!

Mechanical Advantage (page 59)—It was raining heavily, and the man discovered a leak in the roof of his car. He bought several packs of chewing gum, chewed them, and then used the gum as a waterproof filler until he could reach a garage.

Mined Over Matter (page 73)—The sailor used the water hose on the ship to direct a jet of water onto the mine to push it out of the path of the ship.

Mine Shafted (page 69)—He had shredded real silver dollars to produce the silver. One piece was found with the word "unum" (from "e pluribus unum") on it.

My Condiments to the Chef (page 81)—Drug addicts were using his café and dipping their needles into his vinegar bottles because heroin is soluble in vinegar. He replaced the vinegar bottles with small packets of vinegar to stop the addicts from dipping their syringes into the bottles.

Not Eating? (page 79)—His plate is his dental plate.

Not the Führer (page 81)—When the shoes were removed from the body, the man was found to be wearing darned socks. The soldiers did not believe that the Führer of the Third Reich would wear darned socks.

The Office Job (page 70)—This happened in the 1800s. The man had applied for a job as a telegraph operator. Among the background noise was a Morse code message saying, "If you understand this, walk into the office." It was a test of the candidates' skill and alertness. He was the only candidate who passed.

Orson Cart (page 72)—Orson Welles's voice was recognized by the many children who listened to his regular children's radio show.

Outstanding (page 66)—*The Old Farmer's Almanac* had a hole in the top left corner that made it ideal for hanging on a nail in the outhouse.

Paper Tiger (page 68)—It's January and he is writing the date of the year on all the checks in his checkbook to avoid putting last year's date by mistake.

Plane and Simple (page 60)—The boy will be six inches taller than the nail. The tree grows from the top, so the nail won't rise.

Pork Puzzler (page 83)—The man was traveling to a strict Muslim country where alcohol was banned. He placed a small bottle of whiskey under a pack of bacon in his suitcase. He knew that if the customs officials at the airport of entry opened his suitcase, they wouldn't touch the bacon, and therefore his whiskey would be safe.

Publicity Puzzler (page 85)—The man has feet of different sizes—his left foot is 12 and his right foot is 13. He advertises to find a man with the opposite—a left foot size 13 and a right foot size 12. Together they go shopping to find a shoe style that suits them both. They then buy two pairs, one 12 and one 13, before swapping shoes.

Quo Vadis? (page 82)—The archaeologist was excavating a Roman quarry. The ruts in the road leading from the quarry were much deeper on the left than on the right. Since the carts leaving the quarry were much heavier than those returning, he deduced that the Romans drove on the left side of the road.

Rich Man, Poor Man (page 73)—Rich people had bone china that could take the hot tea, but poor people had cheap crockery that would crack if hot tea were poured into it. Pouring the tea first became a sign of prosperity.

Rock of Ages (page 82)—The man was listening to rock-and-roll music through his Walkman headphones in the kitchen. He had his hand on the kettle and his back to the door. When his wife came in, she saw him shaking violently but she heard no sound. She called to him, but he didn't hear. Thinking he was suffering from an electric shock, she picked up a rolling pin and hit his arm, breaking it.

Running on Empty (page 70)—Mr. and Mrs. Jones had had a silly argument. Mrs. Jones stormed out, and the depressed Mr.

Jones had tried to commit suicide by sitting in his car in the garage with the engine running. He passed out, but then the car ran out of gas. When Mrs. Jones returned, she rescued him and they were reconciled.

Rush Job (page 62)—He used the tough tent cloth to make trousers for the miners. His name was Levi Strauss.

School's Out (page 74)—She has just celebrated her 105th birthday, but the computer at the local education authority cannot recognize a date of birth that is more than 100 years ago. Calculating that she is five years old, the computer prints out an automatic instruction to attend school.

The Sealed Room (page 85)—He died from carbon dioxide poisoning, which takes effect before oxygen starvation.

Shell Shock (page 58)—The pea isn't under any of the shells. It's slipped under a shell by the operator as he lifts it. Sometimes the operator places the pea under a player's choice to encourage dupes.

Sick Leave (page 56)—Walter was a newborn baby.

Sign Here (page 68)—He bought two identical signs for his café, but found that he needed two different ones for the two sets of traffic coming in different directions. The two signs said:

"FRED'S CAFÉ Æ" and "¨ FRED'S CAFÉ"

Silly Cone (page 80)—Drinking cups in the shapes of cones were provided at water fountains. Since they couldn't be put down, people had to drink the water quickly. This sped up their breaks.

The Single Word (page 78)—The word was "Guilty." I was foreman of the jury at the woman's trial.

Small Is Not Beautiful (page 85)—Small cars were banned in Sweden because of the high incidence of accidents involving collisions with moose. Occupants of small cars suffered serious injuries, but large cars offered more protection.

Smile Please! (page 68)—The man suggested that they make the hole in the top of the tube bigger so that more toothpaste would be squeezed out each time.

Spies Are Us (page 66)—The German spies wore identical hats with secret information hidden inside the hatband. They entered the restaurant at slightly different times and placed their hats on the hatrack where they could see them. They left at different times—each taking the other's hat.

Stamp Dearth Death (page 82)—The man was a terrorist letter-bomber. He sent a letter bomb, but didn't put enough stamps on it. It was returned to him, and it exploded, killing him.

A Strange Collection (page 66)—The guests are eating pheasant, which they shot earlier that day. The container is for the pellets of lead shot.

The Stuffed Cloud (page 66)—A stuffed cloud, in pilot

slang, is a cloud with a mountain in it. The meteorologist was a passenger on a plane that hit a stuffed cloud. He was killed and had to be replaced at his job.

Superior Knowledge (page 61)—One of the toilet seats had been left up.

Surprise Visit (page 73)—The manager and staff dumped all the trash on the flat roof of the factory so that it wouldn't be seen. Unfortunately, the company chairman arrived by helicopter and landed on the roof.

Throwing His Weight About (page 72)—He was demonstrating how strong the glass was to a group of visitors. He threw himself against it, but it was not as strong as he had thought.

Tittle Tattle (page 66)—A tittle is the dot on an "i".

Top at Last (page 56)—William's name was William Abbott, and the results were given in alphabetical order.

The Tracks of My Tires (page 55)—The woman was the only person in a wheelchair.

Turned Off (page 83)—The man was Guglielmo Marconi, the pioneer of radio transmission. When he died in 1937, all the radio stations in the world observed a minute of silence as a mark of respect.

2020 Vision (page 76)—As he talked to the farmer on the phone, the newspaper editor realized that the man had a slight lisp and that what he had actually reported stolen was "two sows and twenty pigs."

Two Pigs (page 78)—This happened in France. One pig was sold for bacon. The other had been painstakingly trained to sniff out truffles and was therefore very valuable.

Unfinished Business (page 59)—His autobiography.

Up in Smoke (page 80)—In this true story, the cigars were insured under the man's general household policy as named items. He claimed against his insurance company on the grounds that the cigars had been destroyed in a series of small fires. The insurance company rejected the claim, pointing out that he had started the fires to smoke the cigars. He took the insurance company to court and won the case. The judge ruled that the insurance policy covered against loss by fire and that this was what had happened. The man was awarded $10,000. However, as he left the court he was arrested by the police on a charge of arson, based on his sworn testimony. He was found guilty and given a one-year suspended prison sentence.

The Upset Bird-Watcher (page 71)—The ornithologist was sitting on a plane coming in to land when he saw the rare bird, which was sucked into the jet engine, causing the engine to fail and the plane to crash-land.

The Upset Woman (page 55)—He was a mouse caught in a mousetrap.

Vase and Means (page 81)—Bone china was discovered when an unfortunate worker fell into the kiln and became part of the product. Animal bones are used nowadays.

What's the Point? (page 70)—The woman is a carpenter who works on scaffolding at a building site. A conventional round pencil is more likely to roll off and fall.

Who Did It? (page 62)—One of the words that was not rude was spelled incorrectly (for example, "The headmaster is a horribul %$@*&@!"). The teacher gave a spelling test that included the word, and the guilty child spelled it wrong again.

Wonderful Weather (page 58)—The ship was the *Titanic*, which hit an iceberg on a fine night when the sea was very flat. If the weather had been worse, then the lookouts would have seen waves hitting the iceberg or heard the iceberg. (Icebergs make groaning noises when they move.) Unfortunately the iceberg wasn't seen, and the rest is history.

Written Down (page 85)—She is writing along the top of a closed book—on the top of the pages. Any letter with a horizontal line in it is difficult, since the pen tends to slip down between the pages.

Wrong Way (page 77)—The bus from Alewife to Zebedee is always full by the time it reaches the man's stop, so he catches one going the opposite way to get a seat on the bus for the return journey to Zebedee.

WALLY TEST I

Here are the answers to the first WALLY Test.
Be prepared to groan! (page 64)

1. No. He will take his glass eye out of its socket and bite it.
2. No. He will take out his false teeth and bite his good eye with them.
3. You stand back to back.
4. The shadow of a horse.
5. Mr. Bigger's son. No matter how big Mr. Bigger is, his son is a little Bigger!
6. Tom's mother's third child was named Tom.
7. Egypt, Greenland, and Niagara Falls.
8. A glove.
9. An amoeba.
10. A blackboard.

RATE YOUR SCORE ON THE FOLLOWING SCALE:

Number Correct ....Rating
8 to 10 ....WALLY Whiz
6 to 7 ....Smart Aleck
3 to 5 ....WALLY
0 to 2 ....Ultra-WALLY

WALLY TEST II

More answers, more groans! (page 75)

1. Snow.
2. Hide their shovels!
3. It was just a stage he was going through!
4. He was given the Nobel Prize.
5. Mickey Mouse.
6. He changed his name to Exit.
7. At a boxing arena.
8. A hare piece.
9. Don't feed him.
10. To get his feet in (all pants have three large holes).

RATE YOUR SCORE ON THE FOLLOWING SCALE:

Number Correct ....Rating

8 to 10 ....WALLY Whiz

6 to 7 ....Smart Aleck

3 to 5 ....WALLY

0 to 2 ....Ultra-WALLY

Super Puzzles

Adam Had None (page 110)—The letter e.

Appendectomy I (page 114)—The patient was a man who was going on a polar expedition in the first years of the twentieth century. If he got appendicitis in such a remote region, he would die because of lack of treatment, so his healthy appendix was removed as a precaution.

Appendectomy II (page 114)—Shell shock was not recognized as a genuine medical condition during World War I. Sympathetic surgeons often removed perfectly healthy appendixes from shell-shock victims so they could be sent home on medical grounds.

Arrested Development (page 113)—The bank robber dashed to the revolving door and tried to push it in the direction in which it would not revolve.

Arrested Development—Again (page 121)—Bank employees noticed that the two men were Siamese twins. This reduced the number of suspects dramatically.

Bad Trip (page 115)—The anti-drug agency distributed pencils that had "TOO COOL TO DO DRUGS" printed on them. As the children sharpened the pencils down, the message became— "COOL TO DO DRUGS" and eventually, just "DO DRUGS."

Bags Away (page 133)—The passenger's pet dog escaped from his suitcase in the hold and bit through some of the plane's electric cables, thereby disrupting the plane's controls.

Bald Facts (page 111)—After Mary, Queen of Scots, had been beheaded, the executioner held up her head to show it to the mob. The head fell out of the wig.

The Burial Chamber (page 126)—The man was building the burial chamber of an Egyptian pharaoh in ancient times. He built the real burial chamber deep inside a pyramid. He also built another burial chamber that was easier to find that he deliberately wrecked so that when any future graverobbers found it, they would think that earlier graverobbers had found the tomb and taken the treasure.

Caesar's Blunder (page 118)—Since the tides in the Mediterranean are very weak, Julius Caesar did not beach his ships high enough when he landed on the shores of England. Many ships floated off on the next tide and were lost.

Café Society (page 128)—The café owner installed pink lighting that highlighted all the teenagers' acne!

Carrier Bags (page 133)—It was seriously proposed that the British Navy tow icebergs from the north and shape the tops to serve as aircraft carriers. They could not be sunk, lasted quite a long time, and could be cheaply replaced. However, it was too lateral a solution for the Navy high command!

The Cathedral Untouched (page 133)—On a moonlit night, the dome of St. Paul's cathedral acted like a shining beacon to guide German planes during the blackout, so they deliberately avoided bombing it.

The Deadly Drawing (page 120)—She entered the room and saw the chalk picture outline of a body on the floor. It was the site of a recent murder, and the chalk marked the position of the body.

The Deadly Sculpture (page 109)—He lived in a tower on a hill. Being poor, he had no money for materials, so he took the copper lightning rod from the building. He made a beautiful statue with the copper, but soon afterward the tower was struck by lightning and he was killed.

Death by Romance (page 123)—The couple spent their honeymoon on a trip to the Arctic. They stayed in an igloo. The fire melted a hole in the roof, and they died of exposure.

Death of a Player (page 122)—The man was a golfer who absentmindedly sucked on his tee between shots. The tee had picked up deadly weed killer used on the golf course, and the man died from poisoning.

Destruction (page 112)—The body of a very overweight man is being cremated. There is so much fat that the crematorium catches fire and is burned down.

Down Periscope (page 120)—The submarine started at sea, and then sailed into a canal system, where each lock dropped the water level by thirty feet.

Driving Away (page 117)—The rich woman was very near-sighted, but did not like wearing glasses or contact lenses. So she had her windshield ground to her prescription. The thief could not see clearly through it.

Election Selection (page 137)—The successful candidate changed his name to "None of the Above." His name appeared on the list below the other candidates (Davies, Garcia, and Jones). The voters in the deprived area resented all the established political parties and voted for None of the Above as a protest.

The Empty Machine (page 129)—Kids had poured water into molds the size of quarters. The molds were placed in the deep freeze, and the resulting ice coins were used in the machine. They subsequently melted and dripped out of the machine, leaving no trace.

Evil Intent (page 124)—The man happened to put his door key in his mouth (because he was holding lots of other things in his hands). The key tasted of soap. He deduced correctly that his visitor had taken an impression of the key in a bar of soap to make a duplicate key so that he could be burgled.

The Fatal Fall (page 136)—The woman was running in the Olympics in her national relay team. She dropped the baton and her team ended up losing. When she later returned to her country, the tyrannical despot who ran it was so displeased that he had her shot.

The Fatal Fish (page 109)—The man's boat had capsized, and he was adrift in an inflatable dinghy in a cold ocean. He caught a fish and, while cutting it up, his knife slipped and punctured the dinghy.

Generosity? (page 138)—The man robbed a bank and was chased on foot by the public and the police. He threw away much of the cash he had acquired, which caused some chasers to stop to pick up the money and caused a rumpus that delayed the police and allowed the criminal to escape. The people who picked up the bills were forced to give them back or face prosecution.

Give Us a Hand ... (page 124)—The man was a diver searching for pearls in giant clams. A previous diver had had his hand trapped in the clam, and as his oxygen ran out, the poor man was forced to cut off his own hand.

Golf Challenge I (page 123)—The woman's handicap was more than two shots greater than the man's.

Golf Challenge II (page 123)—They were playing match play. The woman won more holes than the man.

Golf Challenge III (page 123)—They were playing darts— highest score with three darts.

The Happy Robber (page 132)—The man was robbing a blood bank. He stole some rare blood that his sick daughter needed for a life-saving operation. He could not have afforded to buy the blood.

The Happy Woman (page 119)—She was playing golf and hit an eagle—two under par and a very good score.

Hi, Jean! (page 129)—The shop owner introduced an electric insect zapper to kill flies and other insects that might land on the food. However, when the flies were "zapped," they were propelled up to five feet, and often fell on the food.

Holed Out (page 113)—The golfer's ball rebounded off the head of another golfer who was crossing the green. The ball bounced into the hole. However, the man who was hit died.

Jailbreak (page 110)—The man knew that his escape would be detected after about half an hour. He escaped at 10:30 A.M. on Tuesday morning just 30 minutes before the routine weekly alarm test, when everyone in the surrounding area would ignore the siren.

Judge for Yourself (page 125)—The defendant sent the judge a cheap box of cigars and included the plaintiff's name card in it!

Kneed to Know (page 115)—The wife of the deaf Thomas Edison used to go with him to the theater. She drummed out on his knee in Morse code with her fingers what the actors were saying on stage.

Lethal Action (page 111)—The Brazilian customs authorities require that all imported fruit be sprayed with pesticides to prevent insects or diseases from reaching domestic crops. They sprayed the hold of a fruit ship arriving from the Ivory Coast in Africa just before it docked in Brazil. They subsequently found the bodies of ten stowaways who had hidden in the ship's hold and who had been poisoned by the pesticides.

The Letter Left Out (page 121)—The letter "W" is left out because it can always be written as "UU"—"double U"!

Lit Too Well? (page 117)—During the blitz in World War II, London was subjected to heavy bombing by German planes. Sussex is south of London. It is on the flight path from Germany, and part of its coastline resembles the Thames estuary. The authorities put lights in fields and in empty countryside to look like blacked-out London from the air. Some German aircrews were deceived and dropped their bombs in the wrong place.

Love Letters (page 126)—She was a divorce lawyer drumming up business!

Message Received (page 135)—Alexander the Great had the envoy's head shaved, and the message was tattooed on the envoy's head. Then, he let the man's hair grow for a few weeks. When the envoy arrived, his head was shaved to reveal the message.

The Mighty Stone (page 135)—The peasant first suggested putting props around the boulder to stabilize it. Then a team of workers dug a big hole around and halfway under the boulder. When the hole was big enough, they pulled away the props, and the boulder rolled into the hole where it was then covered with earth.

Miscarriage of Justice (page 127)—The Italian was Pontius Pilate, who released Barabbas and condemned Jesus

Christ to die by crucifixion at Easter time. Every year Easter is marked by the sale of millions of chocolate Easter eggs worldwide.

The Mover (page 121)—The letter "t".

New World Record (page 121)—The woman's great-great-granddaughter gave birth, so the old woman became the only known great-great-great-grandmother alive. The family had six generations alive at the same time.

Offenses Down (page 128)—The police officers filled in their reports and forms while sitting in marked police cars parked outside the homes of known criminals. Drug dealers, fences, and burglars found it very inhibiting and bad for business to have a marked police car outside their houses. So crime went down.

The Old Crooner (page 137)—The owners of shopping malls found that if they used Bing Crosby songs for the music in the public areas, then they had fewer undesirable youngsters hanging around and less crime was committed.

The Parson's Pup (page 138)—The vicar wears black suits and knows that light-colored dog hairs will show up on his suits, but that black ones will not be noticed.

Peak Performance (page 109)—In the climber's knapsack was his national flag, which he would have planted on the summit had he reached it.

Penalty (page 123)—It was the women's World Cup, and the match was played in a country with strict rules about female nudity or undressing in public.

Pesky Escalator (page 112)—The foreign visitor saw a sign saying, "Dogs must be carried." He did not have a dog!

Poles Apart (page 113)—Before the expedition the explorers deliberately ate a lot of fatty foods and put on several pounds of extra weight so that the fat would serve as food and fuel.

Police Chase (page 128)—The getaway vehicle was a double-decker bus that went under a low bridge. The top deck of the bus was cut off and fell onto the pursuing police car. (This is a famous scene in a movie featuring James Bond, Agent 007.)

Poor Investment (page 124)—The house was in a beautiful clifftop location. But within a few years, coastal erosion accelerated, and nothing could stop the house from eventually falling into the sea.

Poor Show (page 135)—His name was Dick Fosbury, inventor of the famous Fosbury flop, a new high-jumping technique that involved going over the bar backward and that revolutionized the sport. He won the gold medal in the Mexico City Olympics in 1968.

Psychic (page 131)—You notice that the woman is carrying a kettle. It is a very cold morning, and only one of the cars has the windshield de-iced. You deduce correctly that she has defrosted her windshield with the kettle and is returning it to her home before setting off on her journey.

Quick on the Draw (page 119)—The man's wife had played a trick on him. She called him to watch the drawing on TV, and he was unaware that he was watching a video of the previous week's draw. She had bought him a ticket for today's draw and chosen the previous week's winning numbers.

Razor Attack (page 137)—The woman forgot to plug in the razor!

Recognition (page 112)—His Aunt Mary and his mother were identical twins.

Riotous Assembly (page 115)—The institution was a university. Rioting students had raided the geology department and used rock samples as ammunition.

The Sad Samaritan (page 133)—Jim found the full gas can in the trunk of his car. He had driven off and left the motorist stranded.

Scaled Down (page 119)—The butcher had only one turkey left. The customer asked him its weight, and he weighed it. The customer then asked if he had a slightly heavier one, so the butcher put the turkey away and then brought it out again. This time when he weighed it, he pressed down on the scale with his thumb to give it an exaggerated weight. The customer then said, "Fine—I'll take both!"

Sex Discrimination (page 131)—It was found that the female lawyers wore underwire bras, which set off the very sensitive metal detectors.

Shoe Shop Shuffle (page 117)—One shop puts left shoes outside as samples; the other three shops put right shoes out.

Display shoes are stolen, but the thieves have to form pairs, so more are taken from the store showing left shoes.

Shot Dead (page 110)—The woman was a Russian sniper who, during the siege of Stalingrad in World War II, shot several German soldiers.

Siege Mentality (page 132)—Several of the attacking soldiers had died of the plague. Their bodies were catapulted over the walls, and they infected many of the defenders, who were in a much more confined space. The defenders soon surrendered.

Sitting Ducks (page 111)—The woman is an aeronautics engineer. She uses the gun to shoot ducks at airplane engines to test how they handle high-speed impacts with birds.

Slow Death (page 118)—Aeschylus was killed when the tortoise was dropped on him from a height by an eagle who may have mistaken the bald head of Aeschylus for a rock on which to break the tortoise.

Sports Mad (page 114)—The man wanted to record his favorite football team on TV. However, the safety tab on his only videocassette had been removed, and he needed to cover the space with tape.

Stone Me! (page 125)—David slew Goliath with a stone from his sling, and a major battle was averted.

Strange Behavior (page 126)—The man saw a tree lying across the road. He was in Africa, and he knew that blocking the road with a tree was a favorite trick of armed bandits, who then waited for a car to stop at the tree so that they could ambush and rob the passengers. He guessed correctly that this was the case here, so he reversed quickly to avoid danger.

Take a Fence (page 129)—The man had made green paint by mixing yellow paint and blue paint. The blue paint was oil-based, but the yellow paint was water-based. Heavy rain had dissolved the yellow paint, leaving the fence decidedly blue.

The Tallest Tree (page 134)—The men chopped down the tree and then measured it on the ground!

Titanic Proportions (page 121)—One of the reasons why so many perished on the *Titanic* was the shortage of lifeboats. Laws were passed to ensure that all ships had adequate lifeboats for all crew and passengers. One small ship took on so many lifeboats that it sank under their weight. (It must have been overloaded already!)

Tree Trouble (page 126)—The foundation of the wall cut through the roots of the ancient tree and killed it.

Trunk-ated (page 113)—A policeman suspects that there is the body of a murdered man in the trunk. He dials the cell phone of the victim, and the phone is heard ringing in the trunk.

Two Heads Are Better Than One! (page 125)—They were Native Americans who saw a European riding a horse. It was the first time they had seen a horse.

The Unwelcome Guest (page 135)—The couple gave the neighbor a good meal, and when he finished, they gave his scrap-filled plate to the dog, who proceeded to lick it clean. They then put the plate straight back into the cupboard—pretending that was their normal procedure. The neighbor did not come back for any more meals!

Vandal Scandal (page 119)—The authorities arranged for some chips of marble from the same original quarry source as the Parthenon to be distributed around the site every day. Tourists thought that they had picked up a piece of the original columns and were satisfied.

Watch That Man! (page 138)—A picture of the runner early in the race showed him wearing his watch on his right wrist. When he crossed the finishing line, it was on his left wrist. The judges investigated further and found that one man had run the first half of the race, and his identical twin brother had run the second half. They had switched at a toilet on the route.

Weight Loss (page 131)—The doctor running the clinic had noticed that people living at high altitudes were generally thin. The air is thinner, and people use more energy in all activities, including breathing. He therefore located his diet clinic at 8,000 feet above sea level, and the patients found that they lost weight.

Well Trained (page 137)—The child was correct. It was a mail train!

Wonderful Walk (page 112)—During his walk in the woods, the man picked up several burrs on his clothes. When he returned home, he examined them under his microscope and discovered the mechanism whereby they stick on. He went on to invent Velcro.

The World's Most Expensive Car (page 136)—The most expensive car was the moon buggy used by astronauts to explore the moon. It was left there. Although NASA would like to sell it, no one can retrieve it!

Would You Believe It? (page 110)—The second person was underwater, so the block floated up. The third person was on a space station, where there was no gravity, so when the block was released, it floated unsupported.

WALLY TEST III

(page 116)

1. Because it has more geese in it!
2. Because they all have telephone lines!
3. So that he can fit in the small spaceship
4. Exactly where you left him!
5. One. It takes many bricks to build the house but only one brick to complete it.
6. Take away his credit cards!
7. Edam is "made" backward.
8. A mailman.
9. Wet.
10. Take away their chairs.

RATE YOUR SCORE ON THE FOLLOWING SCALE:

Number Correct ....Rating

8 to 10 ....WALLY Whiz

6 to 7 ....Smart Aleck

3 to 5 ....WALLY

0 to 2 ....Ultra-WALLY

WALLY TEST IV

(page 130)

1. Lemon-aid.
2. A lid.
3. The lion.
4. His horse was called "Yet."
5. Get someone else to break the shell.
6. Because he was dead.
7. They use rope.
8. If they lifted up that leg, they would fall over.
9. Wintertime.
10. It wooden go!

RATE YOUR SCORE ON THE FOLLOWING SCALE:

Number Correct . . . . .Rating

8 to 10 . . . . .WALLY Whiz

6 to 7 . . . . .Smart Aleck

3 to 5 . . . . .WALLY

0 to 2 . . . . .Ultra-WALLY

PERPLEXING PUZZLES

An American Shooting (page 184)—This happened during the American Civil War. The men were soldiers in the opposing armies.

The Animal (page 174)—Marmaduke knew that the only animal with four knees is the elephant.

Bad Impression (page 174)—He was a firefighter who, in the course of putting out a fire, sprayed the room and paintings with water. He had indeed damaged the paintings, but saved them and others from complete destruction.

Benjamin Franklin (page 191)—Benjamin Franklin was at one time in charge of the U.S. Mint. Forgery of banknotes was a great problem. He deliberately misspelled Philadelphia on a banknote to enable the detection of forgeries. Unfortunately for him, the forgers simply copied his deliberate mistake.

Buttons (page 167)—Most people are right-handed and find it easier to fasten a button that is on the right through a hole that is on the left. This is why men's buttons are on the right. When buttons were first used, it was the better-off who could afford clothes with buttons. Among this class the ladies were often dressed by maid-servants. The servant would face the lady, and so it was easier for right-handed servants to fasten buttons which were on the lady's left.

Cat Food (page 192)—The man was a TV cable engineer who needed to thread a cable from the back of a house, under the floor, to the front. He released the cat with a string attached to it into a hole at the back of the house. The cat was lured by the smell of the cream and salmon to find its way under the floor to the front of the house. The string was used to pull the cable through.

The Champion's Blind Spot (page 170)—Every other competitor could see someone who had beaten them.

The Cheat (page 194)—For five weeks in a row, the woman gave the man a dollar to buy a lottery ticket on her behalf. Feeling that her chances were nil, he kept the money. Her numbers came up on the fifth week, scooping the $10 million jackpot. She told all her friends and neighbors that she had won.

Checked (page 194)—He used ink that vanished after an hour.

The Coconut Millionaire (page 180)—The man is a philanthropist who bought great quantities of coconuts to sell to poor people at prices they could afford. He started out as a billionaire, but lost so much money in his good works that he became a millionaire!

Color-Blind (page 166)—John was employed by the Air Force during wartime to detect camouflaged enemy positions from aerial photographs. Camouflage is designed to fool people with normal vision. People who are color-blind are much better at spotting differences in the texture and shading of landscape.

The Deadly Suitcase (page 179)—The body was that of the woman's son. They were flying to the USA to start a new life, but she did not have enough money for two airfares. She put him in a suitcase with tiny airholes. She did not know that the luggage compartment would be depressurized.

Disreputable (page 181)—He was born in the presence of his father. His mother died at the birth. He became a pastor and married his sister to her husband.

Disturbance (page 186)—The man had seen a stranger climb into the house through a window. Fearing for their safety, he woke his neighbors up. The "intruder" was a new lodger, who had forgotten his key. The alert man was thanked for his concern.

Dutch Race (page 195)—The race is the famous "eleven towns race," the largest natural ice race in the world. Usually between 12,000 and 15,000 people take part over a course on the frozen canals and lakes in Holland. However, it can only take place after a sustained period of very cold weather. The right circumstances occur around once every ten years. The authorities prepare (for example, by banning factories from discharging warm waste water into the canals) and then give only two or three days' notice of the start of the race.

Early Morning in Las Vegas (page 168)—He had played poker in his room with friends until two A.M. They all had had plenty to drink, and he had failed to notice that one of his friends had fallen asleep behind his sofa. Later, the man woke up and rattled the door as he tried to get out. The gambler let him out.

Fallen Angel (page 184)—The butterfly was made of plastic and was put on a large plate-glass window to indicate the presence of the glass. After it fell off, a man walked into the window and was seriously injured.

The Fallen Guide (page 188)—One of the guides was a book.

Fast Work (page 183)—Marion had been picked up for a ride to the church. She was a member of the clergy and had married the men to their wives. (She was often heard to say that she enjoyed "Marion" people!)

Fine Art (page 193)—The collector was told that the two items were an original Stradivarius and a previously unknown work by Vincent van Gogh. Unfortunately, Stradivarius could not paint very well, and Vincent van Gogh made terrible violins!

Finger Break (page 189)—He was holding a live electric cable. The electricity had paralyzed the muscles in his arm. Her action freed him.

Fingered (page 188)—He did this in case a photograph was being taken of the incident. He reasoned that no newspaper editor would edit out the candidate from a picture but leave his finger in.

Fireworks Display (page 187)—The parents discovered that their baby son was deaf. He reacted to the sight of fireworks but not to loud bangs of fireworks, which were out of sight.

First Choice (page 186)—There had been a spate of robberies at expensive restaurants. The robbers would burst in and take jewelry and money from the people in the restaurant. If you are eating soup then you can quietly drop rings or other jewelry into the soup before the robbers reach your table.

The Flaw in the Carpet (page 185)—Every oriental carpet has a deliberate flaw in its design pattern. Islamic carpet makers believe that to make a perfect carpet would be to challenge Allah, who alone is perfect.

The Flicker (page 184)—The man was carrying a stay of execution for a condemned man who was due to die in the electric chair. When he saw the lights flicker, he knew that he was too late.

Ford's Lunch (page 193)—Henry Ford watched the potential employee eating soup. If he put salt in his soup before tasting it, then he would not employ him. Since the candidate could not know how salty the soup was without tasting it, Ford felt that this indicated a closed mind rather than someone who would investigate a situation before taking action.

Fruitless Search (page 194)—The man was Noah. He knew that if he did not find a second blue-back frog they would become extinct in the flood. Unfortunately, this is what happened.

Gambler's Ruin (page 181)—Syd Sharp was a first-class card player, but he had a bad stutter. Knowing that Syd would be unable to respond fast enough verbally to announce the turning up of matching cards that the game's rules required, Joe challenged him to a game of Snap!

Garden Story (page 195)—The man was in prison. He knew that all his mail was read. He received a letter from his wife asking, "When should I plant the potatoes?" He replied, "Do not plant any potatoes. I have hidden some guns in the garden." A little later his wife wrote back, "Some policemen came and dug up all the back garden but they did not find anything." He replied, "Now plant the potatoes."

Gasoline Problem (page 179)—The man uses the meter at the gas pump to measure out exactly 13 gallons. He puts 11 gallons in the large container and 2 gallons into one of the others.

Gertrude (page 164)—Gertrude, a goose, had been sucked into a jet engine.

The Gross Grocery List (page 189)—The man was a priest who was rather deaf. He asked people in confession to write their sins down and put them through the grill of the confessional. When he handed her back her grocery list, the woman realized that she must have given her list of sins to the grocer.

The Hammer (page 166)—Brenda was blind, and she depended on her Braille manual when using the computer. Alan flattened the pages with a hammer.

His Widow's Sister (page 177)—Jim Jones married Ella in 1820. She died in 1830. In 1840 he married Ella's sister, Mary. She became his widow when he died in 1850. So in 1820 he had married his widow's sister.

Ice Rinked (page 191)—As he approached the woman, he made a sign to ask if she was OK. He put his thumb and first finger together to make an O. This sign is often used in countries such as the USA or UK to mean, "Are you all right?" Unfortunately, the woman came from an Eastern Mediterranean country (such as Greece) where this same sign is an obscene gesture.

Inner Ear (page 169)—She put the girl in a darkened room and placed a bright light near her ear. The insect emerged.

King George (page 184)—It was believed that many cinema-goers would mistakenly think it was the third in a series of movies, and would not go to see it because they had missed the first two. It was released as "The Madness of King George."

The King's Favor (page 165)—The College asked the King to return the painting in six months. Since this was clearly in his power, he agreed.

Large Number (page 169)—The product of the number of fingers on the left hands of every person is zero. It only takes one person to have no fingers on his or her left hand for the product to be zero, because anything multiplied by zero is zero.

The Late Report (page 163)—The man saw the body in the background on one of his holiday photographs. It was two months before the film was developed.

Light Work (page 177)—You set switches A and B on and switch C off. You wait a few minutes and then switch B off. You then enter the room. The bulb, which is on, is connected to A. The cold bulb, which is off, is connected to C. The warm bulb, which is off, is connected to B.

Light Years Ahead (page 177)—Yes—if you look in a mirror, you see light that left your body a finite time ago and has been reflected to reach your eyes. You see yourself as you were—not as you are!

Mad Cow Ideas (page 164)—The Cambodian Government suggested that the cattle be sent to Cambodia and allowed to wander their fields to explode the many mines left over from their wars.

The Metal Ball (page 175)—The disappearing ball was a ball of frozen mercury, which was taken from a freezer. It melted during the course of the act.

Middle Eastern Muddle (page 191)—The agency forgot that people in the Middle East read from right to left. People saw a series of pictures showing the "before" and "after" for the use of washing powder. It indicated to them that the powder made clean clothes dirty.

Mona Lisa (page 186)—The thieves handed the Mona Lisa back but not before they sold a dozen fake copies to gullible art collectors, each of whom believed he was buying the original. None of the buyers could go to the police because they were guilty of buying goods they believed to be stolen. By returning the original, the thieves ensured that they would get only a light punishment if they were caught.

The Music Stopped Again (page 181)—He was an insect sitting on a chair seat during a game of musical chairs.

The Newspaper (page 177)—She slid the sheet of newspaper under a door. The boys stood on either side of the door but on the same piece of paper.

On Time (page 191)—The man is having an affair. Once he has phoned his mistress, he calls the speaking clock so that if his wife should later press the redial button, she will not find out anything he does not want her to know.

One Croaked! (page 175)—The frogs fell into a large tank of cream. One swam around for a while, but then gave up and drowned. The other kept swimming until his movements turned the cream into knobs of butter, on which he safely floated.

Penniless (page 178)—The author's wife was the lady admirer. She had recently received a small legacy and did not want to offend him by offering him money directly.

Personality Plus (page 181)—The man was ambidextrous. He gave two writing samples under different names—one written with his right hand and one with his left hand. The agency gave him two completely different personality profiles.

Poison Pen (page 180)—The sheet of paper on which the letter had been written had been taken from a writing pad. On the previous sheet, the culprit had written his address. This caused a slight impression on the sheet below. The address became visible when the policeman gently shaded the sheet with pencil.

Price Tag (page 166)—The practice originated to ensure that the clerk had to open the till and give change for each transaction, thus recording the sale and preventing him from pocketing the bills.

Rich Man, Poor Man (page 193)—He works at the mint. He makes many millions of dollars a year but draws a modest salary.

A Riddle (page 174)—For the music they played, each band member was paid.

Seaside Idea (page 166)—As he watched his children skimming stones on the water he got the idea for the famous bouncing bombs used by the "Dam Busters" in their raid against German dams. The bombs bounced along the surface of the lakes before hitting the dams and flooding large industrial areas.

Self-Addressed Envelope (page 188)—The man lives in a remote spot ten miles from the bar in the nearest village. If the postman calls on him to deliver any mail, then the man can get a lift from the postman into the village. Otherwise he has to pay for a taxi. He secretly sends himself a letter every day to get the postman to call. The postman does not deliver on Sunday, so there is no need for a letter to be posted on Saturday.

The Single Flower (page 169)—She opened the window, and a bee flew into the room. It settled on the one true flower.

Sleeping on the Job (page 193)—The man was Clark Gable, the screen idol, who took off his shirt in a movie in which he was about to go to bed. He was not wearing an undershirt. So great was his influence that men stopped wearing undershirts and factories making them had to close down. In a later movie, he wore an undershirt and restored it to fashion.

Snow Joy (page 186)—There is a rule in that county that up to six "snow days" may be lost from the school calendar because of bad weather. If the bad weather extends past six days, then each additional day lost must be made up by the school working an extra day—which is taken from the summer vacation. The children were upset that they would now lose precious holidays in the summer.

Souper (page 167)—Her contact lens had fallen into the soup, and she wanted to retrieve it.

Soviet Pictures (page 178)—In a group of ten Soviet officials photographed sitting around a table, there were eleven pairs of feet underneath the table.

The Stranger in the Bar (page 164)—He said, "I am the taxi driver who has been driving you from bar to bar!"

The Stranger in the Hotel (page 167)—She reasoned that if it had really been his room, he would not have knocked at the door but used his key. (She was on a corridor of single rooms, so it was unlikely he was sharing.) In fact, he knocked to check whether anyone was in before using a pass key to enter and burgle rooms.

The String and the Cloth (page 173)—His kite had snagged across some electricity power lines. It was raining. He had been electrocuted. The cloth and string were the remains of the kite.

The Task (page 170)—This is a true story that happened some years ago in New York during a power outage. A telephone exchange in a large apartment building was working on an independent power supply. Many people wanted to phone out, to reassure friends and relatives. They were helped in this by a blind man, who could do a much better job of dialing numbers in the pitch dark than any of them could.

These Puzzles (page 194)—Each puzzle contains a question. The pronoun of the question determines the category. All the "what" questions are in the Aquamarine section, the "how" questions are in the Orange section (together with one "who" question) and the "why" questions are in the Yellow section. (The first vowels of the pronouns are A, O and Y.)

Unknown Character (page 179)—He called the local sheriff, who had never heard of him. He used this as proof of his good character.

Unpublished (page 189)—The manuscript was for the book of the famous play *The Mousetrap* by Agatha Christie. She had requested that for as long as it ran as a play in London's West End, it should not be published as a novel (for fear of giving away the play's secret). Little could she have foreseen that the play would set a world record for the longest run of more than forty years' continuous performances.

Unseen (page 169)—A woman! The man was Mihailo Tolotos, who was taken from his mother at birth and who spent all his life in the Greek monastery of Athos, where no females were allowed.

Unspoken Understanding (page 176)—He gives the cashier four quarters, from which the cashier correctly deduces that the man wants two 40-cent tokens.

The Unwanted Gift (page 190)—The King was the King of Siam, and the gift was a white elephant. The story goes that the King gave the gift of a rare white elephant to those with whom he was displeased and wished to ruin. The elephant was very expensive to keep but was sacred and could not be used for work. Also as a royal gift, it could not be disposed of. This is the source of the expression "a white elephant."

Upstairs, Downstairs (page 167)—It is the First Class restaurant on a luxury ocean liner. Upstairs is out on deck. If it rains, the entire company transfers downstairs and takes up where it left off.

What a Bore! (page 178)—She has a cellular phone in her pocket. Discreetly, she presses a button on it that causes it to give a test ring. She pretends that she has been awaiting an important call that she must take.

What a Jump! (page 173)—It was a ski jump.

What a Relief! (page 185)—It was to collect penicillin, the new wonder drug. It was in very short supply, but American soldiers were given it to protect them against various diseases. The easiest way for French doctors to get hold of penicillin was to extract it from the urine of the GIs.

Where in the World? (page 170)—On a pack of playing cards. The original designs for the Kings, Queens, and Jacks are based on these characters.

Whoops! (page 195)—His host had sneezed, and the guest felt that his dessert had been contaminated. He did not want to eat it, nor did he want to blame his host, so he deliberately knocked the salt into the dessert. He made it look like an accident.

The Wounded Soldier (page 189)—The surgeon had run out of life-saving adrenaline. He knew that the soldier was badly wounded and hoped to provoke a rush of natural adrenaline through the soldier's reaction to his false accusation.

The Yacht Incident (page 188)—All of the people on the yacht went swimming. No one put a rope ladder over the side. They were unable to get back on board again.

WALLY TEST V

Here are the answers to the fifth WALLY test—
get ready to kick yourself! (page 171)

1. Eight days. Each day he takes out one ear of corn and two squirrel ears!

2. The first triangle is larger—one with sides measuring 200, 300, and 400 cm. The triangle with sides measuring 300, 400, and 700 cm has an area of zero!

3. Halfway—after that, it is running out of the wood.

4. In total darkness none of them could see a thing.

5. Mount Everest.

6. On the head.

7. The President would remain President.

8. No candles burn longer—all candles burn shorter.

9. He had one large haystack.

10. Short.

11. A pound of feathers weighs more than a pound of gold. Gold is measured in Troy pounds, which weigh less than the regular Avoirdupois pounds in which items, such as feathers, would be weighed.

12. A bed.

WALLY TEST VI ANSWERS

More answers—more groans!
Or maybe you did better on the last test. (page 182)

1.   1 and 17.

2.   Bread.

3.   Sixes.

4.   In England, it is not usual to bury people who are still alive.

5.   One—after that, his stomach is not empty.

6.   *The Unfinished Symphony* was written by Schubert.

7.   Wrongly.

8.   A hole.

9.   You would be losing 45 cents. I gave you 30 cents in exchange for the three quarters.

10. 12.

RATE YOUR SCORE ON THE FOLLOWING SCALE:

Number Correct . . . . .Rating
8 to 10 . . . . .WALLY Whiz
6 to 7 . . . . .Smart Aleck
3 to 5 . . . . .WALLY
0 to 2 . . . . .Ultra-WALLY

INDEX

INDEX